Once Upon a Pixel

Once Upon a Pixel
Storytelling and Worldbuilding in Video Games

Eddie Paterson, Timothy Williams, and
Will Cordner

CRC Press
Taylor & Francis Group
Boca Raton London New York

CRC Press is an imprint of the
Taylor & Francis Group, an **informa** business

CRC Press
Taylor & Francis Group
6000 Broken Sound Parkway NW, Suite 300
Boca Raton, FL 33487-2742

© 2020 by Taylor & Francis Group, LLC
CRC Press is an imprint of Taylor & Francis Group, an Informa business

No claim to original U.S. Government works

Printed on acid-free paper

International Standard Book Number-13: 978-1-138-49977-5 (Hardback)
International Standard Book Number-13: 978-1-138-49976-8 (Paperback)

Visit the Taylor & Francis Web site at
http://www.taylorandfrancis.com

and the CRC Press Web site at
http://www.crcpress.com

Contents

Acknowledgments

We would like to thank all of our interviewees who have contributed a great deal to this volume and were gracious enough to share their time and expertise. We'd also like to thank readers and colleagues from Melbourne, in particular Leena van Deventer, Rian Henshall, David Harris, and Laura Voss, who provided expert knowledge and help along the way. We thank Sean Connelly, Jessica Vega and the team at CRC Press for all their support in seeing this book to print. We gratefully acknowledge the support of the School of Culture and Communication, at the University of Melbourne, for enhancing this publication by enabling funds for research assistance and copyright support. All images in this work are screenshots taken by the authors or provided courtesy of the companies cited.

Finally, we thank our friends and family. Video games often take a long time to play, and so we thank our loved ones as much for their patience as for their enthusiasm and encouragement for this project.

Authors

Eddie Paterson is a senior lecturer in the School of Culture and Communication, University of Melbourne, where he teaches scriptwriting for performance, theatre, gaming, and new media. He is the author of *The Contemporary American Monologue* (Bloomsbury, 2015) and *Redactor* (Whitmore, 2017). He has returned to gaming in recent years to discover that creative writing is challenging the relationship between gameplay and narrative design.

Timothy Williams is a writer and gamer. His Honours thesis ("'This is Snake'; Interrogating Player Agency Across the Game-Narrative Interplay in *Metal Gear Solid 2: Sons of Liberty*" (2015)) completed at The University of Melbourne explored authorship and player agency in Hideo Kojima's *Metal Gear Solid 2: Sons of Liberty*. His writing focuses primarily on the intersection between narrative and play in writing for games. He is an independent games writer currently working on expanding the creative element of his thesis into a full-length title.

Will Cordner is a writer and gamer. He has an Honours degree in Creative Writing from the University of Melbourne, for which his thesis ("Something to Fight For: An Analysis of Storytelling in *The Last of Us*" (2014)) examined the relationship between traditional and interactive storytelling in Naughty Dog's *The Last of Us*. He is excited to see how this relationship continues to develop in the future and is eagerly anticipating *The Last of Us Part II*.

Introduction
Creative Writers and Video Games

Video games are reimagining storytelling. The fairy tales and fantasies we loved as children are now vast immersive worlds; where stories used to begin "once upon a time," they now begin with a flicker of dots, a playable sequence, and the explosion of a virtual universe. This book explores the possibilities for storytelling and world-building in video games, bringing together the distinct points of view of the player and the creative writer. As authors, we each represent both of these perspectives, and our shared interest in the potentials of video game narratives provides the common ground for our varied gaming histories. Will admires how stories in games can add a new dimension to our playing experience, and his insights on *The Last of Us* (2013) were a catalyst for this project. Tim delights in the scope and vision of contemporary game design, exploring the narrative legacy of one of gaming's most polarizing series, *Metal Gear*. Eddie is a teacher of creative writing who, after a 15-year break, has returned to video games to discover a field that is changing how stories are constructed and imagined. Together, we ask what it means to be a creative writer in this unique space, both now and into the future. How can writers push the boundaries in a medium in which programmers and designers continue to be the driving creative force?

The artistic legitimacy of video game writing has, for many years, been the subject of considerable discussion. It is undoubtedly true that its quality can often leave much to be desired; many games feature clunky exposition and dull dialogue, while others treat story as little more than set dressing. And the unfortunate fact remains, as Anna Anthropy notes, that most games, at least in the Triple-A[1] space, are still about "men shooting men in the face"

---

[1] 'Triple-A' refers to games made by large, wealthy studios, often with development and marketing budgets in the hundreds of millions of dollars.

(2012: 3). But that's not the whole story. There are many games—new and old, from studios big and small—that have fundamentally enriched the relationship between story and interactivity. The past two decades, in particular, have delivered a proliferation of titles that have dramatically broadened the scope of meaningful games storytelling. Naughty Dog's *Uncharted* series (2007–) heralded the studio's investment in deeply immersive narratives, and its first release on PS4, *A Thief's End* (2016), showcased a shift toward more grounded character portrayals and carefully paced narrative arcs. Rockstar, meanwhile, with *Grand Theft Auto* (2001–2013) and *L.A Noire* (2011), has explored, in the span of a decade, two distinct approaches to storytelling in open worlds—the sandbox adventure and the curated narrative—drawing on their lessons from both with the release in 2018 of *Red Dead Redemption 2*, which revealed the potential for absorbing personal experiences to be embedded within vast, profoundly interactive virtual worlds. On a smaller scale, the reflexive narratives of games like *Undertale* (2015), an independent breakout success, continue to examine the tropes, limitations, and possibilities of the form, while micronarratives are more common than ever before in mobile games like *Florence* (2017). The indie scene as a whole is in increasing interaction with the world of Triple-A, with the narrative innovations of titles such as *Braid* (2008) and *Firewatch* (2016) encouraging boldness and ambition from mainstream writers.[2] Indeed, *Dear Esther* (2012) and *Gone Home* (2013) practically invented their own genre—the "first-person walker" (Muscat et al. 2016)—delivering a new kind of game for a new kind of audience. Similarly, industry megahits like *Pokémon Go* (2016) and *Fortnite* (2017), both worldwide cultural phenomena, are known and loved (or loathed) as much by a nontraditional audience as by hardcore fans. And then consider the future—the ongoing potentials of augmented and virtual reality, showcased in games like *Déraciné* (2018), promise new directions for storytelling, while advances in biofeedback and virtual copresence suggest entirely unexplored areas of development altogether.[3] And this is by no means an exhaustive list—it is simply a snapshot of the current landscape, a select few titles that we've been playing and enjoying as a part of our research.

In *Once Upon a Pixel*, we want to both celebrate and challenge the role of writers in enhancing video games as a storytelling form. This is not a

---

[2] "Independent" games are those made by small studios—sometimes even by a single person—with no attachment to big publishers, and usually with comparatively tiny budgets.

[3] The narrative power of this space is being used in a diverse range of fields—from medicine to mining to journalism. Nonny de la Peña's immersive journalism work on "Project Syria" stands out as one method of leveraging this power (2014).

technical guide—you won't find many tips on development—but a book for the fans and the theorists, for those who are interested in how games can create story worlds and narrative potentials, promoting exciting innovations for a new era of creative writing. We include chapters on linear narratives, environmental storytelling, open-world adventures, virtual reality, and the future of narrative design, combined with interviews that focus on the role of the writer as a vital part of the game design process. We speak to people with a range of backgrounds and experiences, from critics to creators in both the Triple-A and independent space: Walt Williams, Brooke Maggs, Brendan Keogh, Anna Anthropy, Damon Reece, and the creative team behind the VR sensation, *Moss*, as well as the multitalented Tomasz Bednarz. Our contributors represent a host of talent from the across the industry; they are video game fans, players, developers, writers, and commentators. And they've all got a story to tell.

These interviews complement our own discussions of specific recent games. We've chosen these games for the ways in which they've changed or developed our conceptions of writing in the medium, challenging and expanding the parameters of interactive storytelling and world-building.

- Five installments from the *Metal Gear* series (1998–2015), Konami Computer Entertainment Japan/Kojima Productions, Director, Designer, and Writer: Hideo Kojima.
- *The Last of Us* (2013), Naughty Dog, Creative Director: Neil Druckmann.
- *The Witness* (2016), Thekla Inc., Designer and Writer: Jonathan Blow.
- *Horizon Zero Dawn* (2017), Guerrilla Games, Narrative Director: John Gonzalez.
- *Moss* (2018), Polyarc, Designer and Writer: Tam Armstrong, and Writer: Shauna Sperry.
- *The Gardens Between* (2018), The Voxel Agents, Narrative Designer/ Writer: Brooke Maggs.

This list reflects our assortment of tastes and interests; we all play a broad range of games. And that is a central philosophy of this book—we are drawing attention to *our* experience, not as objective observers per se, but as deeply invested players and fans. Video games cannot be experienced in isolation; like Keogh, we believe they engage our senses by merging actual and virtual worlds (2018). Our physical bodies are based in Melbourne, Australia; we play games on PlayStation consoles by manipulating DualShock wireless controllers—sometimes with a drink close at hand, or, in Eddie's case, two small children. As Tom Apperley suggests, playing games is as much about the rhythms of everyday life as it is fantastical and technologized futures (2011: 7–8), and in playing and writing about them we are thus linked both to the game world and to the external world, which includes the wider gaming community and the many and varied interactions—conversations with friends, online forums, cross-media content—that inform our contemporary relationships with the medium (Bogost, 2011). We argue throughout this book that it is impossible to analyze worldbuilding and stories in games without also foregrounding the experience of playing; for us, these elements are intrinsically interlinked (see: Apperley, 2011; Bogost, 2011, 2016; Flanagan, 2009; Keogh, 2018; Jayemanne, 2017; Upton, 2015; Swink, 2009). Additionally, we recognize that a focus on story and writing does not comprise the bulk of all modern games. As Keogh asserts in Chapter 4, "not all video game experience can be boiled down to a narrative experience." With this in mind, rather than limiting our analysis to any single component, we instead seek to understand the many intersections between narrative experiences and video game play.

Similarly, we acknowledge the broad range of methods by which games are being made and enjoyed today. The industry has grown consistently in recent years,[4] and as game-making tools become more widely available, unique interactive experiences are coming from many different sources. The independent scene provides vital creative innovation, constantly showcasing interesting new techniques in writing and design. It's also a breeding ground for diversity and self-expression, offering development opportunities with very few barriers to entry. The result is more personal stories and more accessible games. The Triple-A space, meanwhile, provides highly trained professionals with vast resources to create their art; increasingly sophisticated technologies in the hands of multifaceted teams—often hundreds of people—allow for bourgeoning ambitions to deliver powerful global entertainment. Big games are truly big business. But it's limiting to think of the Triple-A and independent scenes as mutually exclusive; in our view, an interest in creative writing for games crosses the borders of all such categories, and it is for this reason that we've chosen this particular collection of titles for closer analysis.

In fact, the line between the Davids and Goliaths has never been more blurred. Even long-running Triple-A franchises, such as *God of War*, which traditionally have paid little attention to meaningful storytelling, are

---

[4]According to newzoo.com's "Global Games Report," gamers spent $152.1 billion on games in 2019, which represents a 9% increase over the previous year (Wijman 2019).

reorienting the core philosophy of their game design to include narrative as a key dimension of the entire process. Indeed, during the development of the series 2018 reboot, a huge banner hung in the foyer of Santa Monica Studios, which read: "Combat, Narrative, Exploration."[5] We are responding to similar such shifts that highlight narrative as a central element in game design.

One of the reasons for this trend is the continued flourishing of the independent sector and its effects on the industry as a whole. Designers such as Anthropy herself are pushing the boundaries of genre and form, experimenting with new and unusual techniques to great effect; her games are widely celebrated for exploring both the complexity of the human experience and the playfulness of the interactive language. And yet the nature of that language remains very much up for debate; not everyone believes that video games are suited to telling meaningful stories. Some industry figures, such as Jonathan Blow, highlight the fundamental disjunction between linearity and interactivity as an insurmountable challenge. Indeed, in 2007, Clint Hocking coined the term "ludonarrative dissonance" to describe that very disjunction as exhibited in *BioShock*, asking how gameplay and narrative can be expected to reconcile within a context that seems to actively divide them. It is a point that has since been made in abundance. We, however, take the view that the context is changing, that such traditional notions of storytelling and world-building are being fundamentally altered. Innovations from writers and narrative designers are impacting the types of stories that games tell, as well as how those stories are being played.

It is those very changes that have been the catalyst for the writing of this book, but our work is also born from the lack of similar resources on creative writing for games. While books on game culture and design are plentiful, this volume expands upon the few existing collections that explore the relationship between creative writing and the play experience. Other works focus more on instruction, often taking the form of development guides for budding designers. These include *Writing for Video Game Genres* (Dispain (ed), 2009), Evan Skolnick's *Video Game Storytelling* (2014), and *The Game Narrative Toolbox* (Heussner et al., 2015). Cultural and theoretical readings, meanwhile, prioritize a broader outline of the industry in a social context: *First Person: New Media as Story, Performance and Game* (Wardup-Fruin and Harrigan (eds), 2004), *The State of Play* (Goldberg and Larsson (eds), 2015), *Video Games and Storytelling* (Souvik Mukherjee, 2015), and

---

[5]As described by head level-designer Rob Davis, during his talk at GCAP Melbourne in 2018, "Exploring *God of War's* Level Design."

Possible Worlds in Video Games: From Classic Narrative to Meaningful Actions (Planells de la Maza, 2017). More recently, personal reflections have provided insights into the careers of industry figures across a variety of disciplines, including players, critics, writers, and designers: Tom Bissell's *Extra Lives: Why Video Games Matter* (2010), Anthropy's *Rise of the Videogame Zinesters* (2012), and Walt Williams' *Significant Zero* (2017). *Once Upon a Pixel* draws most closely on the example of Bissell, who frames his experience as a player of games in relation to his perspective as a creative writer. Like Bissell, we are interested in how the experience of playing games gives new insight into the myriad ways in which games are expanding the definitions of storytelling.

While such definitions are more fluid than ever, it is important to give an outline of how they are commonly applied in the industry today, as well as how we utilize them in this book. The role of the writer in the game design space is changing rapidly, made particularly clear in the increased emphasis on the positions of narrative designer/director as part of the development team. As Brooke Maggs reflects in our interview in Chapter 2, the role of the narrative designer is multifaceted, typically combining the tasks of a writer with that of a game designer, helping to shape the overall direction of an interactive story (see also Heussner et al., 2015). While not all writers for games perform the role of a narrative designer, this combination of skills—a knowledge of narrative rules and conventions alongside game rules and conventions, and how the writing process can enhance the design process—situates creative writing as a key part of the architecture of making contemporary video games. With this consideration in mind, our insights are positioned firmly within what *State of Play* recognizes as the "postescapist" era for video games. Just as the term "gamer" has been redefined to reflect the shifting milieu of the medium, so too has "game developer." Where once writers for games might have been drawn from the (often unskilled or untrained) staff at hand, writers are now frequently invited into the development process at an earlier stage. This is particularly evident in celebrated studios such as Naughty Dog, where Creative Director Neil Druckmann occupies a central role in the conception and construction of the game narrative. With such examples in mind, this book seeks to broaden definitions of both writer and writing in the video game sphere.

Our working definitions of key terms in this book arise from a holistic perspective of the game-making and game-playing experience. Rather than revisit academic debates about the nature of video games as either belonging to the field of narrative media or play, we have chosen to begin from the aforementioned hypothesis that video game texts cannot be analyzed in isolation. We suggest that they involve a complex mix of interactions between:

- The player
- The game rules
- The story world
- The technology

The result is that the techniques of video game storytelling are unique for the ways in which they can combine traditional narrative devices, such as a linear plot or the sequence of events, with the dynamic meaning-making possibilities of an interactive medium. As Mukherjee notes:

> [T]he story, the game rules and the machine code constantly intersect and transform each other as well as the emotions, the muscular movements and the spontaneous reactions of the player.
>
> *(2015: 17)*

Therefore, while traditional narrative may refer to the specific ways in which events are situated, sequenced, and represented (Herman, 2009: 9), the interactive presence of the player complicates and broadens the storytelling potential of the medium. Additionally, story worlds for games are frequently nonlinear in design, and so branching and modular narratives, and nontraditional approaches to character and situations, are also possible ingredients in a game's creation (Bode and Dietrich, 2013).

And yet, as Bissell notes, while the use of "story" in games is multidimensional, the term is commonly misunderstood, both by designers and players, as equating to explanation and/or narration—the notion that the more the game *tells* the player things, the more complex or "whole" the story is (2010: 40). With such misconceptions in mind, we argue that the definitions of video game storytelling need to be expanded to include the ways in which story moves beyond mere narration or accumulation toward more playful and expansive meanings. We are interested in storytelling in games that foregrounds narratives shaped through play, resulting in unique "narrative spaces" (Jenkins, 2004) or fictions shaped through dynamic interactions, rather than preset narrative events (Planells De La Maza, in Bigl and Stoppe (eds), 2013). The result of this broadened conception is that writing for games can now be considered not merely in relation to other forms of creative writing—the prose novel and feature screenplay, most obviously, or even forms with a larger degree of potential interactivity, such as theater—but on its own unique terms.

More specifically, we suggest that our understanding of two major concepts—"storytelling" and "world-building"—must be expanded when considering video games as a form of creative writing. Whereas "story" traditionally relates to plot in a fictional universe, in games the idea of "storytelling" also relates to emergent or "ludofictional" narratives created through play.[6] The limits of the fictional universe can be expanded by the player's interactions in the game world and how game rules, events, actions, starting points, environments, conflict, and objectives intersect within a dynamic system (Planells de la Maza, 2017: 123). These ludofictional elements are the basis of possible game worlds, and these worlds also include slippages between the "real" world of the player's physicality and the "virtual" world of the game.

As such, whereas world-building usually figures as an *ingredient* of narrative in fictional worlds, world-building in games is far more complex. As defined in *The Game Narrative Toolbox,* world-building incorporates the development of all the "details of the world where a story takes place, including its history/ geography, peoples/races, governments, science/technology, religions, and languages" (Heussner et al., 2015: 243). This definition recalls the more passive concept of "lore," a staple of fantasy and role-playing games, but world-building is also influenced by aspects of a game that arise actively during the play experience, including environmental storytelling, audio-visual design; game mechanics, such as combat or movement; camera point-of-view (POV); and interactions with player avatars, AI, and NPCs (nonplayer characters).

As an example, let's consider Rockstar's *Red Dead Redemption 2* (2018), which provides a useful overview for understanding how these terms might practically function in the play space. Players control hardened outlaw Arthur Morgan in a fictional version of America's Old West. Storytelling here fits the standard three-tier model for open-world games: a main story, side quests, and dynamic, player-driven exploration. Players advance the main story by confronting specific characters or locations in the game world, which provide the opportunity to complete missions and quests. These individual stories combine over the course of the game into a complete narrative. Focusing solely on the main story recalls the experience of playing a linear game. Side quests, meanwhile, are smaller optional adventures that add texture to the game world without directly affecting the main story. These missions often prioritize more eccentric characters and varied mechanics, providing a chance

---

[6]Planells de la Maza provides an expanded definition of "ludofictional worlds" in his 2017 book, *Possible Worlds in Video Games: From Classic Narrative to Meaningful Actions.* The term has a clear through line to Hocking's ludonarrative dissonance and goes a long way toward reconciling the problems Hocking highlights.

for the player to perceive more of the narrative flavor in the game's digital space. That space, which in the case of *Red Dead Redemption 2* is impressively vast,[7] is open to exploration as the player desires. Such exploration occurs outside the authored narrative, during free-roaming gameplay in which much of the game's emergent world-building takes place. A player can choose how and when to spend their time, either partaking in a range of predesigned activities—hunting wildlife, camping, playing poker—or simply existing in the world. Rockstar has created a dynamic space in which this latter alternative is not only feasible but highly fulfilling, as the environment and its AI inhabitants react variously to both the player and each other. The results can be wildly unpredictable—random encounters will lead to a seemingly endless array of short play stories, such as fighting off a deadly animal, getting lost in a storm, or being involved in a saloon brawl. These moments are essentially nonscripted and instead emerge organically from interactions between the game's manifold systems. In fact, outside of dialogue and authored missions, most of the game's world-building is in this way hidden.

The result is a clear encouragement for the players to create their own narratives. This is a common attraction of the open-world genre. In *Red Dead Redemption 2*, Rockstar utilizes the mechanical implications of its western setting to promote a steady and deliberate tone in gameplay. Arthur is languid and heavy in his movement, realistically affected by terrain, and dynamic weather systems force the player to plan ahead. Navigating the environment on horseback takes time—gallop for too long and Arthur will be bucked off—and players who neglect to care for their steed will soon be in need of another. In isolation, these mechanics suggest a challenge to tradition; Triple-A games tend to promote action above all else. But it's with a clear narrative alignment that these same mechanics combine to establish a deliberately contemplative tone, which reflects the game's actual story. Arthur is a tired man slowly coming undone from the hard and fast life of an outlaw.

In this way, *Red Dead Redemption 2* presents multiple story interactions that together form an entire ludofictional world, with every individual play experience forming another possible version. Storytelling techniques in video games are expansive and varied, and it is the role of play in bringing them to life that is the important point for our discussion. *Red Dead Redemption 2* represents the current peak of the Triple-A model, and yet these very same interactions— between the story, the player, and the game—are evident even in the smaller, but no less innovative, games featured in this book.

---

[7] It takes almost 2 hours to walk across the game's entire map.

Chapter Outlines

The following chapters are the result of a collaborative writing process. This introduction, the closing chapter, and the conclusion were all cowritten, and the interviews were conducted by the three authors. As per our overall philosophy—that stories in games are connected to the interaction between physical, virtual, and technological bodies—we also include three chapters on an individual play experience, in which we each explore a specific area of interest. Considered overall, this book thus takes the form of a dialogue between the subjective experiences of play and a social commentary, combining to underline the diverse nature of analyzing storytelling and world-building in games today.

We begin by speaking to Walt Williams, renowned writer of *Spec Ops: The Line*, about what it means to be a creative writer in the industry today. We ask him about the challenges and possibilities of working with large teams and how best to apply lessons from the independent space. Walt offers terrific insight into why the work and expertise of writers must be more readily acknowledged in Triple-A games.

Our interview with Brooke Maggs in Chapter 2 provides an alternative perspective, as she gives an insight into working as a narrative designer on smaller, more experimental titles. She reflects on her lifelong love of fiction and the ways it has influenced her career in games, and ponders her transition into the Triple-A scene with her recent move to Remedy Entertainment in Finland.

This interview is followed by our first personal analysis, as Will leads an exploration of linear storytelling through a close reading of Naughty Dog's *The Last of Us*. He considers how a combination of traditional narrative techniques and the unique possibilities of interactivity can promote meaning that transcends the limitations of these apparently disparate creative fields.

Will's chapter is followed by a chat with video game theorist, Brendan Keogh, who's own reflections on *The Last of Us* and other modern games—most notably, *Spec Ops: The Line*—argue for a player-centric approach toward narrative. Brendan suggests that the creative limitations of Triple-A production make true storytelling innovation possible only in the independent space.

Innovation, in fact, is the theme of the next chapter, as Tim gives an overview of the unique storytelling legacy of Konami's *Metal Gear* series, highlighting the impact of the legendary Hideo Kojima on writing for games. Tim considers specific moments from the series in which the two potentially dissonant models of narrative and gameplay intersect.

Tim's look at Kojima leads into a discussion with Anna Anthropy about self-expression through video game storytelling. Anthropy is a designer, developer, writer, and teacher, and she reveals the power of nontraditional interactive experiences to communicate meaning.

Eddie then considers how new techniques for games writing are embodied in open worlds, drawing closely on his experiences with two recent games, *Horizon Zero Dawn* and *The Witness*. He explains how creative writers are bringing together linear narrative techniques with ludic immersion and environmental storytelling to enhance the experience of gameplay.

We further explore these new means of storytelling in our Chapter 6 interview with Damon Reece, discussing how online games have created new avenues into emergent narratives, and highlighting the importance of non-structured encounters as a vital part of contemporary game worlds. Damon dissects the vocabulary of the industry, suggesting a greater push toward a codification of narrative best practices.

Our next chapter, "Virtual Reality and the Narrative Frontier," looks at new storytelling practices in recent games. We investigate *The Gardens Between*, an independent hit on which Brooke Maggs worked, and dive into VR fairy tale, *Moss*, examining its coalescence of old and new narrative techniques.

Our look at *Moss* is supplemented by an interview with Polyarc's Lincoln Davis, Tam Armstrong, and Shauna Sperry about the unique experience of writing for virtual reality, and how *Moss* navigates the largely uncharted waters of VR storytelling.

This discussion of new technologies provides the platform for our final interview, a conversation with Tomasz Bednarz about the possible futures of storytelling and world-building in games. Tomasz gives an insight into his unique background and his views on a techno-utopic world.

As we move between play experiences to our interview discussions, we want to highlight the diverse trajectories of game experience and the range of storytelling possibilities for the medium. We believe most of all in the vital role of creative writers in shaping, challenging, and enriching video game design and culture, now and into the future.

1

Interview with Walt Williams

Walt Williams is an award-winning writer for Triple-A video games, including *Spec Ops: The Line* (2012) and *Star Wars Battlefront II* (2017). In 2017, he released his first book, *Significant Zero: The Fight for Art and Soul in Video Games*, which recounts his fascinating career in the industry to date. Walt currently lives in Louisiana with his young family.

In this interview, Walt reflects on different approaches to designing narratives for games, advocating a philosophy that includes story from the very beginning of the process. He argues that, at least in the Triple-A space with which he is most familiar, a clear leading voice encapsulated in the modern role of a "creative director" is essential in ensuring that each disparate piece of the design puzzle can fit together. Yet he also acknowledges the realities of the video game business, citing the economic constraints of big-budget productions as a powerful deterrent to anyone seeking to challenge the norm. Reflecting on his work on *Spec Ops: The Line*, he bemoans the frustrations and hurdles of the Triple-A system, highlighting the notion of player agency as one of the most powerful illusions in gaming today. Even so, Walt remains hopeful that, with a realignment in recent years toward more varied and personal story experiences, particularly in the independent scene, the role of the writer in games can continue to develop in interesting and meaningful ways.

EP: We're interested in the space for writers in Triple-A games. How has the industry changed in this regard while you've been working in it?
WW: There definitely is a space for pure writers in this industry. Clearly, there is because there are quite a few of us. It's a role that's becoming more readily available as teams begin to realize that writing is a specific, studied skill set. I always compare writing for games to

architecture—you use words to build a narrative structure that will support the many disparate pieces of a video game and keep them from collapsing on top of each other. However, the Triple-A games with the most celebrated stories usually have a creative director who personally identifies as a writer and who takes a hands-on approach to crafting the narrative. Those games have a better chance of elevating their craft because the literal creative boss has the authority to harmonize story and design. That's not the case when you're working with just "pure writers." Sometimes, writing and narrative are treated like a plaster cast, forcing a shattered, useless bone to hopefully knit itself back together, whereas the best game stories understand that narrative is the bone, the entire skeleton, giving their game structure. This is because writing can be seen as a constraint by other disciplines, such as design, art, etc. These disciplines traditionally control the form of a game's vision, and they bristle at ceding any of that control to people who just "put words on paper." But, if we want a game to have a truly impactful narrative, then design and narrative have to be built in tandem. It's like building an arch out of stone—you place a stone on the right, then a stone on the left, over and over until both sides come together at the top, creating that perfect balance of weight and pressure that makes it stand firm.

EP: What are the qualities that these sorts of creative directors, these architects, bring to their work that is slightly different from a more design-focused creative director?

WW: A design-focused creative director, in my experience, is going to be focused on the player experience entirely. The sandbox they're building is all about how someone is going to play with it and express themselves. That's not to say that a story-focused creative director doesn't care about that. They do. For example, someone like Ken Levine cares about that sandbox aspect of his games, because in games like *BioShock* and *System Shock*, you're playing with all the different systems to find different ways of solving your problems. Player expression is important, but the narrative aspect comes in because there is a vision beyond simply what the player is going to be doing in the game. This vision plays into themes, narratives, arcs, and a message of what the game is trying to say. There's a cinematic aspect that design focus does not necessarily draw from. A narrative-focused creative director is able to think narratively in a visual space, a space that's cinematic and theatrical at its core. We have many thousands of years of storytelling to learn from and lean on. Having an intimate knowledge of that structure is an important aspect of being a narrative creative director that a design-focused creative director does not necessarily have in their personal toolbox. I came from writing first, and I then learned design by working in games for 13 years so I always approach a game from a cinematic angle. I'm looking to create a logical series of progression, conflict, and escalation that is driven by character choices (player-driven or predetermined) that will maximize the player's emotional reaction at any given time. Design is looking to create a system by which the player can choose what to do during gameplay and thereby maximize their personal emotional reaction by feeling as if *they* authored the flow of the experience. It's a very different kind of thinking.

EP: I suppose it also lends to a certain type of production process. Are there moments where you feel like the Triple-A production model is really frustrating to work within?

WW: We have a tendency to put the world and the experience before the story. That's frustrating to me as a writer and world-builder because it feels like we're putting the cart before the horse. I like to find the core of the story first, the emotional core that is personally resonating with me and with this experience. That gives me the themes I want to tap into and the emotional arc I want to create for the player. At that early stage, I'm thinking more about the feeling that I want the player to have than exactly what's going to cause that feeling. That emotional core is the seed from which the world grows. As the world grows, design, art, and story can take the fruit of that work and expand upon it, until you have a whole ecosystem that feeds upon and fuels itself. Once you have that, then you can find the actual beat-by-beat details of your story. Unfortunately, Triple-A has a tendency to focus on the world first and that's because that's the biggest aspect. Who the character is or what the character is doing isn't important at the start of development. We just need to figure out everywhere they're going, everyone they're talking to, and everything they're going to be doing—we don't need to figure out why, or who they are, that's later. Up to this point, that strategy has worked perfectly fine, and by perfectly fine, I mean it hasn't tanked a game. A great story can elevate a fun game to being a masterpiece, but a shitty story has never stopped people from buying and enjoying a fun game.

Accepting that there are different ways to come about crafting these big games and building these worlds is difficult. Obviously, Triple-A video games have a hard time branching out into the "totally new," and we instead focus down on what we know how to make. We work within these familiar structures over and over, and a lot of that comes from the technical aspect of our industry. If a developer spends 20 years making first-person shooters, they won't suddenly start making racing games. The design, feel, and balance of these experiences are totally different. That's not to say making a jump like that is impossible; you'd just need more research, experimentation, and development, all of which comes down to time and money. Modern Triple-A games already have astronomical budgets, and they're only growing larger. Increased cost means increased risk. So, we stick to what we know. Instead of branching out, we double down on a formula that works and polish it to a perfect shine across multiple iterations. Or beat it endlessly until nothing is left but a bloody, soggy pulp, depending on your point of view. The more technologically advanced the game becomes, the more difficult it is for that game to branch outside of a very thin track because you have too many moving pieces, too many timelines, and too many budgets. I can't tell you how many times I've rewritten dialogue for a cutscene that was finished and had to match new words to lip syncs of old lines that were completely different. I'll put a video of a cutscene up on a screen in front of an actor and say, "okay, here are the new lines—watch your lips and match it to the lips that are moving on your character's face." These guys are professional actors so they pull it off and you never even notice, but we had to do that a lot on *Spec Ops*. This is why a lot of experimental stuff is coming from indie teams. Smaller teams, smaller budgets. There's just as much risk involved, because an indie team doesn't have the safety net provided by Triple-A publishing, but you can turn a sailboat a lot faster than an oil tanker. Instead of a 300-person team, you have ten people who can more easily interface and experiment.

TW: One of the advantages of Triple-A development would seem to be that more resources allow for more expansive game worlds and stories. In *Spec Ops*, for example, there are branching endings. Is there one ending that you consider canon? Is "canon" even an applicable term for interactive narratives?

WW: I don't know that there's an ending that I consider canon. I've always said that he [Captain Martin Walker, the game's protagonist] is dead, and that is true—I think he is dead. How you want to interpret that is up to you; he could be physically dead or he could be emotionally/ spiritually dead. Ultimately, if a game with multiple paths and multiple endings is written with thematic intent, then all the endings can be considered canonical, as they will still speak to the same theme. With *Spec Ops*, in every ending, Walker is destroyed by what he's been through. The choice comes down to how that destruction manifests through your guiding hand. Can you accept blame for your actions in destroying this character? Will you cast blame off on the developer? Or will you decide it's just a game, it ultimately means nothing, and you can keep shooting people until we make you stop? The choice is about examining your own culpability and expressing those feelings, or lack thereof. But, thematically, it's all the same, so it doesn't really matter what ending you have. In that regard, canon in games does exist.

WC: Have your thoughts on that changed in the 6 years since *Spec Ops* was released?

WW: I certainly used to think that there was one specific ending, and now I think they are all the same. I definitely didn't feel that way when I wrote it. Back then, I hated branching endings, because they don't provide a definitive conclusion to the experience. If a player knows a game has multiple endings, they will either change how they play the game so they can get the "best ending," or they will just play through it multiple times to see every possible ending. These days I suppose more players just watch all the endings on YouTube. Instead of creating a personalized experience, multiple endings make players worry about the content they might be missing. With *Spec Ops*, I wanted to write a branching ending that felt definitive, no matter which ending you chose. First, I made sure that the ending wasn't determined by the player's choices throughout the rest of the game, so that it wouldn't affect how they played. Second, I wanted each ending to feel so personally definitive that players would beat the game, put down their controllers, and say, "I'm satisfied. I don't need to see anything else." Some people actually did that, and it's the biggest compliment I've ever gotten.

WC: You suggest in *Significant Zero* that there's really only one kind of Triple-A game story: there are bad guys, you're the good guy, you save the world. How successful was *Spec Ops* in challenging that template, and where were you unsuccessful?

WW: I think *Spec Ops* was very successful, in that the game called out the lies we build around the Triple-A hero narrative and the violent mechanics that support it. In regards to simply getting the vision of the game across to the audience, it was very successful. As to it having a lasting effect on that audience, it was a total failure—absolutely 100%. People felt very bad for playing shooters for about a week, and then a new *Call of Duty* came out. But that's okay! The goal of *Spec Ops* wasn't to fundamentally change the face of video games. The goal was to create a shockingly personal piece of art that resonated with its audience, and we did that, as evidenced by the fact that we're still talking about it 6 years later. Our industry is always looking for validation and trying to find proof that games are more than just games, to justify our choice to make and play them well into our adult lives. But the world has already accepted games as a legitimate artistic medium. The question of "are games art?" still pops up from time to time. But more often, that question is replaced by "what constitutes a game?" Our medium has reached the point of cultural relevance that people now attempt to control it through definition and exclusion. As terrible as that is, it's also a sign that we are well past the point of needing validation. Of course, any attempt at defining the medium is idiotic, the last resort of frightened and fragile people. Games are art, and art exists solely to facilitate the expression of the artist. Video games are nothing but a vessel and should never fit any paradigm or mould.

TW: Speaking of that idea of self-expression—one of the things we're most interested in is the unique ways that games can tell stories. I agree that games are perhaps not the *most* effective medium for telling stories, but I also wonder if there aren't some stories that *only* games can tell?

WW: The most effective way to tell a story, bar none, is me telling it to your face with my mouth while you're chained to a chair. Second, books... maybe, if you can get someone to sit down and read the whole thing. It's certainly not games. When you add audience interaction to the mix, you give your audience a wealth of opportunities to emotionally divorce themselves from the experience, because instead of empathizing with a character they become that character. As a writer I don't believe that there are stories that only games can tell, but there are certain types of stories that are more effective inside of a game format. Taking *Spec Ops*, for example—you absolutely could tell the story of *Spec Ops* as a film, but the main theme of *Spec Ops* is about the player's culpability in choosing to take part in interactive entertainment.

It's about not turning your eye away from the messy parts of that experience and the actual effect that it has on the people you're controlling. *That* part would be lost if you took *Spec Ops* from a game to a film, but you could still adapt that theme to one of the culpable voyeuristic audience. There are shifts that any adaptation to another medium would require but that would ultimately change the theme of the game. The types of narratives that are made most impactful by being a game tend to be the narratives that directly speak to the fact that you are playing a game, and that's interesting.

TW: So interactivity can distance the player? What are your thoughts then on player agency? How does it manifest in different kinds of video game storytelling?

WW: Player agency is a really nice bullet point to put on the back of the box. The metaphor I always use is eating a slice of pizza. You can eat with your hands, or with a fork and knife, or you can roll it up into a tube and shotgun the whole thing. But ultimately, no matter how you choose to eat it, you are still eating exactly what someone else decided you should eat. That is the full extent of player agency, because players can only do what we allow them to do. A book has more "player agency" than a video game. You can read it front to back. You can read it out of order. You can cut out all the words and rearrange them into an entirely new book. You can use the pages to start a fire. You can rip off the cover, fold it into a boat, go outside, and watch it float gently down a stream. That is true agency. There is no real agency in games, not in the way we claim. What we present in video games is an illusion of power. We give you three highly controlled, preauthored choices and tell you you're a god because you picked A, B, or C. It's safe because player agency cedes total control to the developer by removing the risk that is inherent in all true choices. Players don't want to be in control, they just want to feel like they are. They trust us to give them only choices that matter—to remove the chaff, the ineffectual moments, the margin of error. For me, I don't care about having agency when I play a game. Day-to-day life is enough agency for me, thank you very much. When I play a game, I want to be transported into someone else's world. I want to experience their vision and design. Art is a way of stepping outside myself and experiencing the world through other people's eyes. When you look at the games that we celebrate, games like *Grand Theft Auto* or *Red Dead Redemption*, they don't have real player expression. They have the story, and then they have the world. If you decide you want to play the story, then you're playing exactly the story they created. There's no fake sense of branching or player agency. Or look at the stuff that Naughty Dog puts out. No one cares that their games are entirely linear because they're brilliantly told stories filled with true emotion. When your story is immersive and true, players don't need a fake sense of agency. We empathize and project ourselves onto characters, even those we don't control. Humans have been doing it since the moment we started telling stories. We have myths, we have legends, we have all these stories that we have told to help us explain the universe but that also allow us to project ourselves onto them. The idea of player agency feels like such a narcissistic way of looking at narrative and story in games. Like the only way we can truly experience the world through someone else's eyes is to inhabit them so completely that they cease to be another person. Kind of defeats the purpose. Part of me thinks this hyperfocus on player agency has led to the toxic entitlement that comes from certain parts of the gaming audience.

WC: So if true player agency is an illusion, what tools does a writer have to bridge that distance between the game story and the player? What do you think of cutscenes, for example? How do they impact things such as player involvement, pacing, character arcs, and the building of a game world?

WW: Cutscenes are a wonderful tool. Game designers don't like them because they don't have any control over them. That's a joke. Kinda. Every game has cutscenes, whether the game wants to admit it or not. Even if the cutscene stays as the player's point-of-view and the game needs to tutorialize something—the player gets knocked down and then the villain says, "Next time you should DODGE when I PUNCH you." That's a cutscene. If you take control away from the player in order to force information through their eyes and down their throats, no matter how briefly, you are creating a cutscene. This dislike of cutscenes actually comes down to a dislike of narrative control and the sense that cutscenes are ruining the immersive experience. It's a very sociopathic way of looking at immersion because humanity did not spend its entire existence reading books, watching films, looking at paintings saying, "I just don't get it, I don't understand or empathize with this person at all—if only it was me." The idea that you can only be immersed in the game if you're in the eyes of the character and you have total control is very weird. We spend most of our time in our own bodies doing our absolute best to not be in total control of ourselves. Imagine a first-person game where you're actually just looking at your phone the whole time because you don't want to be doing what you're doing. Immersion comes from the dramatic experience; it doesn't come from this unconnected sense that you are the character. That's just another tool in the dramatic toolbox.

You know what I think? I think cutscenes with quick time events in them are the worst. Let me just enjoy what your cinematic team put together. I'm playing *Spider-Man* [developed by Insomniac and released in 2018] right now, and it's great, I love it. There are some top-notch action sequence cutscenes in it, and when I'm just completely absorbed in it they're like, "QUICK! PRESS SQUARE!" Don't do that to me. Action is still immersive if it's done well by talented artists. I don't need to push a button to feel like I'm actually Spider-Man; I already do feel like that because you made a great game.

EP: We're all actually playing *Spider-Man* right now. We were just talking about it prior to talking to you.

WW: I rarely play games when they come out. I've got a kid, I've got work—I will pick it up when I get time. But, honestly, it's been a real joy to play a game at the same time as everyone else in the world. To feel like we're all having this discovery and experience together has actually been really great. The fact that you guys are playing it right now too—that's it, we're all in that exact same moment of discovery in this thing. I'm glad we can be sharing this emotional experience together even though we didn't know it.

EP: Yeah, it's really lovely. Walt, I wanted to ask—are there moments where you're not necessarily surprised by what's happening narratively in a game but where you feel a similar joy; moments in the semirecent past where you've really enjoyed the ambition of the developers or a moment of narrative design that really works?

WW: Yeah, actually, in the new *God of War* game. I've always been very uncomfortable with Kratos as a character. I played the first three games, and it got to the point where it jumped into Poseidon's POV while Kratos gouged his eyes out with his thumbs, and I was controlling Kratos' thumbs with the joysticks. I'm clearly not opposed to violence in games—I make them—but it was trying too hard, so I took it out and returned it to the store and I hadn't played a *God of War* since. The idea that Kratos is a now father didn't change my opinion of him, and it didn't draw me to the game. But I saw a lot of people having really strong emotional reactions to the game, which for me is the sign of something worth experiencing. Now, I'm a new father, so when it comes to parent-child stories I currently empathize with the parental POV. When I started the new *God of War*, it kind of turned me off because the relationship Kratos has with his son is the exact opposite of my relationship with my daughter. The relationship was cold and distant. To me, it felt like this was the same old Kratos, only grumpier. Then, I reached the point in the story where Kratos and Atreus are hunting a warthog for the second time, and Kratos kneels down beside his son and gently puts a hand on his shoulder. It was a moment of actual tenderness, the type of tenderness that I feel when interacting with my own child. That small act of tenderness spoke to me. This, right here, is what I want—I want a game where people care. If it's violent, let it be violent, but I want a game where characters actually care. I want a character who is physically tender, who can express that remorse and emotion and their full dimension to the world and to the characters around them.

There's another moment when he goes to dig up his old weapons, which he has thematically/ceremoniously buried, along with his past. When he does so, Athena appears in the shadows behind him and says, "you cannot change. You will always be a monster." Entirely to the credit of the actor and the animation team, Kratos' face just drops, and his body sags in complete resignation. The actor delivers two words: "I know," delivered in the most defeated, heartbroken way. It still sticks with me because, like tenderness, the other thing I crave in Triple-A games is vulnerability. I want characters who are broken and know it. I want to see our humanity expressed through trials and tribulations, not ignored because it might ruin the illusion of empowerment. These two moments were enough to get me through the rest of the game. They were so real and so outside the paradigm. We're so afraid of making our characters vulnerable because we think players will be turned off by the idea that they aren't a 100% badass. We see vulnerability as the amount of physical damage you can take, not the fears and scars that drive your decisions. Being emotionally vulnerable and fragile doesn't fit into the paradigm of what a player-character should be, and that sucks because that's what I want from my art. There's a place for escapist entertainment, absolutely, but I also want things to be able to be more meaningful and to explore weaknesses. Certainly, if I'm going to spend five and a half years writing that shit,

I need something real and emotionally true; otherwise I'm going to stab my eyes out. Writing a tough-as-nails uberman whose only real weakness is how much he loves killing bad guys isn't exactly creatively challenging or fulfilling.

WC: A lot of this sounds a little depressing for writers. In fact, you've said before that "writing video games has made me a worse writer." Could you speak a little more about the interactions between writing for games and for other media?

WW: The thing that I noticed while writing *Significant Zero* was how much my internal barometer for feeling out narrative had become skewed and broken. I had spent so many years writing around gameplay beats that I'd grown accustomed to putting a story on pause every couple of pages so the audience could take control and play the game. There's so much when you're writing a video game that you don't have any control over: what something is going to look like, how characters are able to interact with the world, how players are going to interact with each other. This goes right down to things like having a character run their hands through their hair—"we can't animate hair"—or having them in the shower—"we've only got one model and they're always wearing these clothes." When you're doing that kind of writing exclusively, you train yourself to ignore certain aspects of reality in common life. So when I began writing my book, I didn't have art or design to lean on. I had nothing but my words and a broken sense of narrative rhythm that had withered and died after 13 years. Eventually, after enough times of putting ideas out there, I decided I'm not going to bother getting excited about writing things that are going to be glossed over, ignored, or thrown out because they're not seen as necessary to the all-killer-no-filler mindset of certain games. Slow moments are the first thing to get cut because they're not important; a slow moment is just putting more time between the player and the gameplay. So you stop thinking about narrative rhythm in that way. Dialogue is another thing—everything has to be so short, so clipped, so focused on delivering information and exposition that you lose your ability to think in natural conversational ways when writing. I sit down to write dialogue for something that isn't a video game, and everyone is just saying, "Hey, so here's the thing that we have to do." Everything just becomes terrible video game dialogue designed to constantly remind the player of what they're meant to be doing at any given moment. You don't get moments where characters just talk about nothing unless it's during traversal gameplay, in which case it just gets cut off early once you arrive. If it's not specifically moving the plot or gameplay forward, then it doesn't matter in a video game, and that's depressing as a writer.

EP: Are those limitations universal in all video game writing, or does it depend on the type of experience you're trying to create? You've spoken previously about writing independent games—what elements there might translate across to the Triple-A space?

WW: I tend to refer to my indie game work as self-indulgent. When I say self-indulgent, I simply mean that it is fueled entirely by what I want to see in a game that I haven't been able to create in the Triple-A space. Sometimes, the reason is production constraints, or I'm a contract writer and that's not the direction the people in charge have for the game. These are perfectly valid reasons, but as an artist there are things that I want to explore, so I have to find my own avenues for that. Indie games are one of the avenues I have found. The thing I'm working on right now, which I think could have had a lot currency in the Triple-A space, is a new way of marrying character to gameplay. When we design gameplay, regardless of character or story, we always design gameplay elements strictly as a player empowerment tool—there are going to be obstacles you come across that can only be solved by this specific gameplay tool we've given you. You are going to hit this button, and it is always going to cause this action that will have this effect. What it comes down to is, "did you push the button at the right time? The wrong time? Did you push the buttons in the right order?" We have to create characters that match the action rather than the other way around. It's as simple as, "this is a shooter so the player will shoot guns, and that means the character has to be someone who is good at guns, because whenever the player presses this button they will fire their gun like a person who is good at guns." The character is only an expression of the gameplay, never the other way around. During gameplay the character vanishes entirely. They only serve as your hands, ears, and eyes. As someone who plays and makes games, that's not very exciting. So the indie game I've been working on, called *23 Skidoo*, is trying to solve that by having gameplay be a direct extension of a character's personality. The base layer of gameplay is turn-based tactical combat. However, instead of focusing the tactics on character movement and ability, the tactics are driven by each character's quirks and reactions. A simple example is two characters with a bad relationship might refuse to stand within two tiles of each other. More complex is a character whose reflexes sharpen when they're scared, so being surprised by an enemy will cause them to react with a lethally effective attack and then run away in terror. Where the system becomes quite tactical is when you begin playing these quirks off each other to cause a chain reaction of action and reaction, all driven by your characters' egos, fears, hubris, etc. Relationships inform actions that inform reactions that inform new relationship dynamics. It's emotional jazz with guns, where the narrative of interpersonal relationships is taking place in the gameplay. Thus, characters are continuing to grow and express themselves throughout a player-controlled moment. The entire idea for *23 Skidoo* originally came about because I got tired of people asking when I would make another military game. My response was always, "did you play *Spec Ops?*" Because if you have, you probably understand that I am very critical of the genre. Then, one day I responded, "the only way I'd ever make another military game is if it were inspired by Catch-22 or M*A*S*H*... wait a minute, could I actually do that?" And from there, it grew into *23 Skidoo*, a tactics game where you manage the personalities of an insane ensemble cast in order to achieve success through military combat.

EP: So character and gameplay need to carry equal weight. There has to be a push and pull there that promotes each aspect within the context of whatever the game world is trying to say and whatever the player is trying to do. As players, we recognize that games need to have challenges to move the story and character forward, but often what drops out is the emotional progression along the way. I think what you're speaking about is absolutely true, in the sense that you not only need player challenges but you also must have emotional challenges that link in with those.

WW: Absolutely. The only emotional challenge that traditional design cares about is how to keep a player engaged. I've had design meetings where people ask a question that essentially boils down to, "what is going to be the player's personal reason to interact with our game?" My cynical response is always, "because they've already bought it." We've already sold them on the experience. We don't have to spend time easing them into the idea of it. We can toss them straight into the conceptual pool, and let the world simply be what it is. The emotion created by a game's story isn't about driving engagement; rather, it is the response to engaging. Players have already signed up for the journey—now you get to take them for a fucking ride. In *Spec Ops*, Walker is a character who solves his problems with a gun. We played that out logically for what that does to him and the people around him, and people were like "oh wow, that's messed up." Well yeah, that's what happens when you solve your problems with a gun; you're a person who has a completely skewed worldview. If you allow the story of the game to not only embrace truths but also enhance them and bring them to the forefront, then you can guide the player on a true emotional journey. The Triple-A space is so afraid of doing that because we feel that the only emotional journey our players should go through is the ones that they choose to define for themselves or that have the broadest range of appeal. We tend to hold up Triple-A video games as the peak of what the medium can be because it's the prettiest, the most expensive, and they sell the most. Thankfully, we've got developers like Fullbright and Campo Santo who are taking the entire visual language of Triple-A games and making games about weird awkward isolation and romance in the woods. Clearly, they're all doing great, because you don't get bought by Valve if not.[1] Change is there but it's coming out of the slowly developing indie world. All the good writers in the industry have known this secret, but it's about having the freedom to go off and do it.

TW: That freedom—I wonder if it's embodied by some of those "good writers in the industry," like Hideo Kojima?

WW: I found the *Metal Gear* series to be impenetrable, and I've never gotten very far into any of them. I was completely unaware of the original *Metal Gear Solid* games when they came out on PlayStation 1 because I was too busy playing *Final Fantasy* games. With that said, I think what I've seen of Kojima's work is insane and I love that. I want more insane. *Death Stranding* is an entirely new level of insane, and I can get in on the ground floor as a stand-alone experience and understand it—or not understand it, however it may be. There is a certain level of distance to Kojima's personality in that he self-mythologizes. He is very good at building a cult of personality around himself that doesn't come across as entirely egotistical. The way he presents himself, and so much of what he puts into his art, is about the things that he loves and the things that he's inspired by. When you play a Kojima

---

[1] Valve acquired Campo Santo in April 2018.

game you are seeing Kojima's influences, you are seeing what he loves and you are seeing what interests him in the art he consumes. Those influences are varied, dense, weird, and sometimes impenetrable, but there are levels that can lead you to appreciate things outside of video games. That's rare in a video game. Most of the time, when I play a game, the only inspiration I see is from another, popular game. It's like, "okay I get it, you really liked *Half Life 2*, but I don't need to play another train ride homage." So much of Kojima's inspiration comes from outside of video games, and I think that's superinteresting.

TW: Speaking of inspiration—let's circle back around to your inspiration for *Spec Ops*…

WW: The truth is I tried to read of *Heart of Darkness* once in high school and I got halfway through and thought, "this is really racist, I don't want to read this anymore." As it turns out, you can piece together most of those stories just from the cultural zeitgeist of what exists in our collective heads. This is an interesting thing with me, and I don't know other people who research like this. I grew up in Bible Belt Louisiana, with a family that was fairly religious but not restrictively so. I didn't get to watch R-rated movies growing up. There are films from that era that I've never seen but that I'm still hyperaware of due to the discussions around them. Another inspiration for me was GameCube's *Eternal Darkness: Sanity's Requiem* (2002). I never played it, but it's a game that people loved and they talk about a lot. It's kind of a scary ghost game, and it will pretend like it erased your game, or the menus start messing with the player, or it'll start lying to you. I loved that. So I said, let's do that with our loading screen and have our game physically turn against the player—let's play with the culpability of the audience. If I'm inspired by something like that and I know where it comes from, I specifically do not watch it or read it or play it, because I don't want to be influenced by the way that they did it. It inspires an idea, and I want to do it my way without knowing how someone else did it. My fear is that if I become too familiar with the inspiration, I'll just end up creating a pale imitation. But if it remains a seed of inspiration, it can grow in my mind to something new and unique.

TW: I think that's a fascinating method. Do you think it helps to keep you original?

WW: I think it helps in ensuring that what you're trying to do remains in your voice. Ultimately, I think that's the most important thing. As game developers, we spend so much time hiding our voices. Who spends their life trying to become an artist just so they can then never be seen within their work? It's such a self-deprecating medium because we reach this point of actually creating something out of nothing, and then we convince ourselves that what we want is less important than the desires of some 15-year-old who might buy it for $20 at GameStop. It's heartbreaking. People actually pay us to create art that will be played by millions of people. It's difficult to reach that point in your career, and we've done it. It's our time to shine, but we curl into ourselves—*ah, player choice…* When I play a game, I don't care about my player choice; I want to be guided down your path.

TW: You've said that change is coming, albeit slowly. How do you think it's all going to play out?

WW: The Triple-A industry can absolutely change, but I don't expect it to change during my time. What we're seeing right now in the industry with indie studios like Fullbright and Campo Santo is the dawn of a new era similar to what began the Triple-A industry in the early 1990s, with companies such as id Software. In another 30 years, games like *Firewatch* are going to be the Triple-A games, and people will be saying, "gosh, we've been playing emotionally heartfelt first-person world exploration games for 20 years now, why are games so uncreative?" The indie scene becomes the Triple-A scene that becomes the retro scene that becomes the Kickstarter revival scene, and it all circles back around. There are those of us that see the change, but we know it's not going to happen while we have our hands in the industry. But that's fine. I'm happy now. I've found peace. I make stained-glass windows, I have a kid, I garden—it's wonderful. And occasionally, people pay me to write video games.

2

Interview with Brooke Maggs

Brooke Maggs is a narrative designer, writer, and researcher from Melbourne, Australia. She has worked on acclaimed independent games such as *The Gardens Between* (2018) and *Florence* (2017). In 2017, she won the MCV Pacific XBOX Creative Impact Award for her work in the games industry. She is currently based with Remedy Entertainment in Finland, where she has been working as a narrative designer on *Control*, released in August to widespread critical acclaim.

Brooke has a background in short fiction, and in this interview, she provides a unique insight into the challenges and possibilities of transitioning into writing for games. We ask her about the crossover between traditional and interactive writing, and in particular about what games designers can learn from conventional storytelling methods. She reflects on working as part of an independent team, highlighting the complexity of bringing even a small, textless game, such as *The Gardens Between*, to life, and ponders the comparisons to her future at Remedy in working with a whole team of dedicated writers. In looking ahead, she also considers how traditional narrative techniques might be utilized in combination with emerging technologies to create new story experiences. Brooke wants video game writers to explore different genres through different means, and speaks with excitement about the range of future possibilities for interactive storytelling.

Will Cordner: Brooke, you're a writer for games and for other media too. But what are the kinds of game stories that most interest you as a *player*?

Brooke Maggs: I really enjoyed *Her Story*. The premise of the game and the game mechanics worked really well. At no time did you feel any disconnect between what you were doing and the stories and the characters. *Hellblade: Senua's Sacrifice* is also pretty incredible. It doesn't hold your hand with the gameplay. It lets you figure things out over time, and even though the gameplay mechanics aren't super original I think their treatment—the artwork and the sound—it's really simply done. Having boundaries and restrictions on what you can do in development really makes for a creative game sometimes.

WC: So you're drawn to experiences without those all-too-common barriers between the player and the game? Like with *Her Story*—there are no walls between you and the game, are there?

BM: No, and I really enjoy games that do that. *L.A. Noire* was another good one. But in terms of that disconnect, it's funny, because sometimes I don't mind it, but other times I think, "oh god, I'm Lara Croft, why am I collecting a million and one tokens to do this?" What broke me out of the whole *Arkham* series was when I started playing *Arkham City*, and literally one of the first things I had to do was run around rooftops and collect Riddler Tokens. I'm like, "I'm the Dark Knight—I don't want to collect Riddler Tokens."

WC: Some of those frustrations are unique to the player-game relationship; you don't necessarily find those same issues in other forms of storytelling. On a more positive note—how can games tell stories and construct worlds in ways that other media don't manage quite as well?

BM: Well, those incidental story moments. "Emergent narrative" is the word. In *Half Life*, you could run down the hallway past this security guard and not pay him any mind. Or you could see him—I think he's clutching his stomach and reaching for the first aid kit on the wall—and it's just this incidental thing that's happening, but you as the player can choose to engage with that or not, which might give you a different view of the narrative. When you're writing and designing story for games, the player ultimately needs something to do. That's where pure game design and designers start. What are the mechanics of the game? You can jump, you can shoot, you can modify your weapon, you can get superpowers, you can get different recipes to cook a meal. But then when you have narrative on top of that it's like, "well, game design says that you need to unlock five new recipes later on—what is the context for that?" The context is that your mum comes home with her recipe book and hands it over to you because you've been doing so well cooking that she wants you to move on to the family's secret recipes. There are sometimes links to gameplay progression that are there before the story, or sometimes the story will dictate them. Ultimately, it's when they work together that things work really well.

WC: You've touched on some of the unique challenges of the process of writing for games. What was it like to come into a game design space as someone with a more traditional writing background?

BM: Well, I started as a writer before I jumped into games. I had my professional writing and editing qualifications, and I was teaching games and game studies at Swinburne. I got the job on *The Gardens Between* based on a twisted fairy-tale I'd written, and so I thought I was coming into this for my ability to write prose. I guess I should have realized quickly that that wasn't going to be what *The Gardens Between* needed, or what any game needed. How do you tell a story when you have no text or speech? The technical and design decisions can get solved, and then they turn to narrative and go, "so narrative…" or vice versa. Narrative can say, "so this beautiful thing happens," and then tech and design go, "hmm, that's not going to work in our environment." Usually, writers in games get good at working out what is technically and not technically possible, and that's a part of the craft as well that perhaps new writers from other mediums don't realize. If we don't have text or speech, it's probably not super important that we explain the entire backstory. I would be asked for lengthy explanations, and I'd often say that I don't think people are thinking about it that much. No one asks in *Lord of the Rings*, "why are there orcs in the world?" So often I found the simplest explanation is a good one too, and people are happy to go with it as long as it doesn't feel too out of context. So with Lara Croft, for example, you have her journal; that interface is designed specifically to keep the illusion going.

EP: So it seems writing on games might mean doing very little writing of prose; it's more about connecting together other ways of moving a story on, or other ways of providing context. Is one of the real skills for a games writer then to take text and simplify the story? We have this conception of a writer as someone who comes in with all these narrative possibilities and wants to play them out, but the other option is that they become very editorial in the approach, which is equally important.

BM: Yes, and also to ask the question, "what makes an interesting experience?" as opposed to, "what makes an interesting story?" Those two things are important. But it's not always advantageous to write a lot. I call myself a narrative designer mainly because, while I can write, I have not written a lot for games in the sense that my words haven't found their way into the finished product. My words are incredibly important, however, because they communicate the story to the development team, and the development team has to know what the story is in order for it to clearly feed into all their disciplines. One of the main things a narrative team can do is be very charismatic about the story. Games, a lot of the time, are plot driven—"go here, get this, move over here…" I think what often gets left out is the question of how the character is *feeling* at that point in time. That's a double-layered question, because it's how is the *player* meant to be feeling and how is the *character* meant to be feeling? And it's okay if those two things are different, but we just need to be sure.

TW: It sounds like those are some of the great advantages of working in the independent space—being able to speak closely with people in different roles and ask those sorts of questions. You're about to go and work with Remedy in Finland. What do you anticipate some of the challenges in a bigger studio might be?

BM: Well, it's easier to communicate with a smaller team, first of all. Remedy, the last time I checked, is 140 people, if not more. There's a whole team on *Control* that does visual effects, and there's a whole team that does motion capture and the movement of the characters, and then there's a whole team that does lighting. Those jobs can actually be done in isolation of the story, which is interesting to me. They know what the story is, what the general feel of the story is, but I don't think they're paying as much attention as the narrative team, which is why you have a narrative team in the first place. I'm really looking forward to working with more than one writer. When I was there for my residency, I got to see the other writers inducted into the game at the same time. It was really cool to see what these seasoned professional writers in games had to ask about a project they're just being introduced to, which I wouldn't have thought of coming from an indie space, because those things just wouldn't even be on the table. They would say things like, "can we come up with puzzles?" "What are the key cutscenes in this scene?" "When do we need scripts locked down for voiceover?" The production of the narrative is larger, and there are a couple of things that come from that: one, you're working with more people, and two, your narrative touch is more moving pieces, which means you have a more solid deadline but also, because narrative is the most flexible, it's often the one that accounts for things disappearing, like whole levels or parts of the game that just can't exist anymore due to production. It becomes harder to convey the important points of the story. There are probably some people who would work on the game and not necessarily know the whole story from beginning to end until the game's finished and out the door. Their job is just too busy to have that kind of information. So as much as that would have other writers clutching their pearls, you just kind of understand that it takes a long time to move a character's hand five different ways.

WC: I'm sure being part of a bigger writing team will expose you to all sorts of different approaches and philosophies, too; lots of people coming from a variety of backgrounds, a combination of the new and the old. In your speech at GCAP 2016, "Advocating for the Story," you reference Christopher Booker's "seven basic plots." How do you think video game storytelling challenges, or perhaps reinforces, more traditional models of storytelling?

BM: I can start with reinforces. "The Hero's Journey" is the easiest one to pair with gameplay. You start out as a noob.[1] Your main protagonist doesn't know what they're doing, but they have a quest to go on because some inciting incident happens—their father dies, they inherit a sword, etc. Then they go on a great quest to become more powerful and to confront a greatest foe. They get wise teachers along the way who give them information. All of this is like quest giving and collecting and leveling up, so that plot works really well. "The Hero's Journey" has a plot push—you're always going forward on this quest. And we always want to encourage the player to keep going, to keep moving. We don't want them to stop and put down the controller and never come back. In the "Voyage and Return" model, there's not so much of a push, which was actually really good for *The Gardens Between*. Games can be interpreted as, "bang bang, shoot shoot, rush through"—you have to get really good at pressing buttons in a certain order at a certain time. That's really intimidating for people who don't really play games. I think people who play games and know indie games well enough don't have that feeling, but I think the general public who are not necessarily into games would think that. One of the things I loved about *Florence* is that it was a romantic comedy, in a way. I think games could use more romantic comedy. I think games could use more "Rebirth" plots, different kinds of plots. I would love to play a soap opera! I don't know where I can play a soap opera right now. But the question becomes, "cool, we want a soap opera game, but what does the player *do*?" So then you have to think of a mechanic. It's a soap opera where you are trying to rescue your lover from the jaws of death, and there's this really cheesy voice over all the time that might say, "and then you discover your long lost twin." And then cut, fade to black, open, new scene—the player has to have a conversation with their long lost twin and somehow get some information. So you can see I'm immediately going to plot to figure out some gameplay. I think that's how you try and make a game out of those plots, but they're harder, which is probably why I haven't done as much.

---

[1] 'Noob' is a slang term for an unskilled player.

WC: So you've been able to apply some lessons from your background in more traditional fiction to your writing for games. Does it work the other way around? Has your writing for games taught you anything for your other writing, or are those skill sets too dissimilar?

BM: No, I think they're similar. For me, I have a lot of trouble finishing my fiction, and I think it's got to do with the fact that I am really plot heavy. I've just finished a short story actually, which is amazing because I never finish. But I think ultimately what I struggle with is doing character, which is funny, because I will tell my friend about all of these things that are going to happen in the story, and she would just kind of go, "yeah, yeah, yeah, but what does all that *feel* like?" Which is hilarious, because when I go to games I'm always the one saying, "that's cool, we're going to shoot people, we're going to do all of that, but what are we feeling at this point in time?" I have a lot of trouble pulling that through in my own fiction. On the plus side, it makes my fiction pretty visual. I like to design my stories, and I often put together a mood board and do a few character profiles every now and then. I know plenty of authors do that. I think that's a bit "gamey" too.

EP: That's interesting, that need to keep coming back to the interior world of a character. When you're writing prose, you really have to remember that. A character might have thoughts, and you actually have to tell the reader. It's a different type of audience reaction, I suppose?

BM: It is because I think when I'm writing prose, I sometimes think, "oh, I don't need to say, 'I'm feeling this or she's feeling that,' because, surely it's obvious." But you're right. Some people go, "um, I need some explanation about all of this." To me, those sentences feel really heavy-handed, but they're actually fine for that format, and I have to make that switch.

EP: I think in games, a lot of the time, like you were saying about *Her Story*, you're constructing narratives and possibilities alongside the audience, and when that works really well, they're kind of happening together. In fiction, that doesn't always happen. As a reader you're having your hand held a little bit more. It is a kind of process that's slightly different, I think.

BM: Yeah, and also I guess it depends on how the game is put together. If you're reading a police procedural, you're always trying to put things together in your head, but when you're playing *Grand Theft Auto*, you can just go and do your own thing or you can follow the path of the narrative. And both are pretty legitimate. But I also think there's a difference between the player-experience story and the story in the game. I think you can design and write for both, but I don't think they should be confused. Some people say that *Tetris* has a narrative, but I don't agree. I think there is a *play narrative*, a play experience. You definitely feel tension throughout that—you either win or lose—but it's not like someone sat down and authored the narrative. So I think they're two different things, but I think it's important to know both of them. As a writer, as a narrative person in a game, you can just plant things in the world for people to make up their own stories, and that's great, that's part of the fun. But some games really just take you from story point to story point, and it's still a story that holds together. So it ultimately depends on what experience you're creating, and what kind of narrative game you're making, and not that one's any better than the other.

WC: It seems like a lot of your experience in the games industry so far has been as a kind of narrative problem solver, someone brought onto a project later in development to work on story. Can you picture it the other way around? Imagine that you are the fundamental creative cog, right from the outset, and then the game designers come on board later to solve the mechanical problems. Could that structure even make sense in games?

BM: Yeah, I think it could. I really like that idea. I think I would have to have some idea of what I wanted the player to be doing. But I could probably write a story and then meet with game designers and say, "how would you turn this into a game?" That would be interesting. I think they're different skill sets, but I think they're very related to one another. That would be really cool, actually.

WC: It's like story-first design. One example that springs to my mind is Hazelight's *A Way Out* (2018), which really suggests this idea of finding gameplay to fit narrative. "Gameplay" there is really about filling in the gaps. What problems can that philosophy pose? And how might they be solved?

BM: Well, with *A Way Out*, it's about their [Leo and Vincent, the game's dual protagonists] friendship and their relationship, and sort of having to solve their differences in order to do something. And I think there is a bit of a narrative suggestion in those mechanics. It's really interesting to have these two main characters together. And that was even with *The Gardens Between*—we thought, should we have them follow each other? Should we have just Arina leading or should Frendt sometimes take the lead? And what does that say about the story? And we gave them both their own unique abilities to give them a unique personality. And then, because we didn't want one necessarily privileged over the other, we had them sort of swapping paths at different times. So there is an equality to those characters, which speaks to the friendship themes of the story. But it would be interesting if you had these two main strong characters with very distinct personalities, and then added mechanics in where they had to help each other. Man, you're making me think so much. You could position the player as just one of those characters—you have to pick—or you could be standing back and controlling both of them, and then you might be making decisions about how you want their relationship to play out. So you can have different layers of influence that you can give the player in that game. The important thing is that the narrative and the gameplay moments are linked. You don't want to go, "story, story, story, 'Oh, I get to press something now,' story, story, story..." Unless it's a game that's very much in that genre, like the Telltale games, which I really enjoyed even though it's pretty minimal game mechanic interaction. The story works well to make the choices important, so when I do interact I'm like, "oh my gosh, yes!" And then I make a choice.

EP: You've spoken a bit about finding new opportunities for storytelling in a broader range of game experiences, like different genres and mobile gaming. Let's talk about possibilities for storytelling in VR. How do you imagine that technology, or really any kind of new technology, can influence story in games?

BM: So I've done some work in VR storytelling. I worked with Opaque Space, with their very early prototype, *Earthlight*, and also with VRTOV on one of their documentaries. VR is really interesting because at the moment the technology is good but it's still catching up. And what I mean by that is it's probably not accessible for everyone at the moment. People probably still have a few hang-ups about putting the VR mask on. But also when you're designing a story for VR, people are seated, and they're moving their head around a lot, so there's kind of more physical comfort of the player you need to take into account. The play sessions can't be too long; people's necks can kind of get really sore.

EP: Yeah, mine gets really sore. It's difficult to play for long periods.

BM: Especially with glasses. It's really crap. But having said that when I have used VR, I've been really blown away by the fact that I could look down at something on the floor, bend over, and pick it up. That was cool, I was just like, "my god, I'm in this. Like, I am *in* this!" And I felt that way with *The Turning Forest* as well, which was VRTOV's VR fairy-tale. It was glorious, because you were just placed in these scenes of beauty that you could look around at and really enjoy. So there are some key things that you can do in VR that you probably can't do in any other media just yet. I mean outside of probably theater, because theater crosses over with it so much. For example, you can track where the player is looking, and so if the player is looking at a character, the character can meet their eyes, which is really different. [Game design guru] Rob Morgan does a great talk about signaling players to their positions by having the VR world, or AR [augmented reality] world rather, react to them. So someone will look at them and acknowledge that they're looking at them, and even that's enough to create that fantasy of being in the space. Also, if you can track where a player's looking… Rob Morgan uses the example of—if you look at another character's backside, the character can turn around and go, "why are you looking at my bum?" And so something like that can just make the player go, "oh, I'm actually here, I better be a bit careful." What I love about VR is the social cues that you can play with, where you're held a little bit responsible for your actions and what you're doing in the world. That's really interesting. I think the challenge of VR games is making the mechanics interesting. And it's not easy. I spoke to someone at Double Fine who worked on the *Psychonauts* VR game, and he said they literally had to reengineer the whole thing from the ground up. Like, it's a completely different technical process. But I think the storytelling potential of that is yes, bringing players into the world a little bit more, but through those social cues, which is interesting. And it doesn't have to be an action-packed thing, either, because I think VR can be quite powerful as it is. It can be very understated and still be really cool.

EP: I think the idea of social cues is a really great point.

BM: I think there's probably more opportunity in AR and MR [mixed reality] at the moment. It's very much similar to what we have on our phones and things like that. There's an app that does purely audio stories, where you can move left or right to acknowledge a direction. Or I can even imagine spoken word stories, where you could create dialogue options, which I think would be awesome. We could have characters who are artificially intelligent and come up with their own dialogue. That's what I'm excited about. People are talking about AI and saying robots can write books, which they probably can, but I think what's actually interesting is when we write the artificial intelligence that will tell the story. So it's like a step removed. Like if you can design your own set of patterns or rules for an artificially intelligent system, and then implement it, which they kind of do for games already, where you have enemies with certain AI to behave in a certain way, like if the player dodges, then they do this, etc. For me I would love to see those as personality rules. So, for example, if the player insults a character three times, then the character will now no longer talk to them. It might even be less exciting as a writer, but what you would do is you would create the data that you would give to the machine that would teach the machine how to be your character. I think it will be interesting when you can create a profile of a character that's your character, but then you can talk to that character and they can tell you things that are completely in character but that you would never have thought to write for them. That would be super cool. Like, for better or for worse, I could have a conversation with the protagonist in my short story. Which might be limited, but it'd be super interesting.

EP: And it does push in different genre directions as well. You've talked about other different types of plots. You can imagine other possibilities arising from that too.

BM: Yeah, definitely. Essentially, the AI would act like the game master of a tabletop role-play. You would tell them some key ideas for some plot points in this particular plot arc. It's a romantic comedy—there might be a meet-cute, there might be someone spilling coffee, there might be an identical twin—and then they throw up these plot points. If the narrative tension is getting low, then we'll introduce the identical twin! But I still think actual people probably do a better job than robots right now. But I think that's interesting. I don't know if we'll get there or not, but I'd be excited about what you could do as a narrative designer for that. I also think that we probably don't push the boundaries enough of designing narrative tools for writers and narrative designers. There are some out there that are quite good, but in terms of actually implementing the story… yeah, I think that's often left up to the tech people to sort of hard code and put in using the tool that makes sense to them. But I think as more advanced narrative tools come out, like Fungus and things like that, that's interesting because then people don't have to have a tech background to tell interactive stories. So that could be really cool.

3

Something to Fight for
The Last of Us *and the*
Language of Linear Games

Here's How This Thing's Gonna Play Out

I think about *The Last of Us* every day. Like the parasitic virus that kick-starts the plot, Naughty Dog's masterpiece burrows further into my conscious-ness with every passing moment. On the surface, it's nothing special—just another violent video game about zombie-like monsters and the end of the world—but it's what lies deeper, from the perspective of writing for games, that keeps me coming back. As a piece of interactive storytelling, *The Last of Us* makes deft use of the various strengths of its form, and in this chapter I will provide a fresh perspective on how those strengths manifest in the relationship between story and gameplay.

> Our medium is still so young and we're figuring out the language of how we can tell stories using interactivity, and we feel like there's so much more we can still do.
>
> – *Neil Druckmann*, Creative Director, *The Last of Us* (2013)

Whereas Tim's discussion of the narrative legacy of the *Metal Gear* series applies traditional theory to some of the most elusive works in the medium, and Eddie, looking at *Horizon Zero Dawn* and *The Witness*, finds oppor-tunities for new storytelling in the advent of the open world, here I will consider a more familiar dialect of Druckmann's "language"—the linear action game—and how storytelling in *The Last of Us* reveals it to be far more complex than is often thought to be the case. Naughty Dog's creative process emphasizes the alignment of gameplay systems with traditional narrative techniques, and Druckmann himself has reflected frequently in recent years on this particular philosophy of development.[1] I want to explore how the divergent properties of the old and the new alike—of conventional literary practices and the untapped potentials of interactivity—can combine to breathe new life into an apparently tired formula.[2]

I first got my hands on *The Last of Us* about 3 months after its June 2013 release, borrowing it from a friend (and his PS3—thanks Dave!) in a barely containable whirl of anticipation. I'd followed the drip-feed of news closely since the initial reveal—rarely have I dived so deep into prerelease fanfare—so to finally get hold of a copy was extremely exciting. I set up the console in haste, glancing down at the game on my coffee table as if only to confirm it was really there. The cover art is fairly generic—the two lead characters, Joel and Ellie, stand armed for a fight in the ravages of a postapocalyptic world. As Kotaku critic Kirk Hamilton noted at the time, "we've been down this road before" (2013). And yet that is partly what had me excited. I knew—*knew*—from watching snippets of gameplay, from reading and rereading countless adoring reviews,[3] that this was going to be something truly special. Naughty Dog had drawn fresh blood from that most tired narrative corpse, the "zombie game," to rejuvenate our understanding of what a linear Triple-A experience can be. Or so I'd been told. At that moment, sitting alone in my darkened living room as the game continued to load, it all lay ahead of me, waiting to be discovered. Apparently the campaign would take 15 hours. I was ready. The title screen had just appeared. I put down the case, picked up the controller, and started the game (Figure 3.1).

Make Every Shot Count

The precredits sequence of *The Last of Us*—the "prologue"—is as memorable a start to a video game as I've ever played. Tom Bissell calls it "one of the most astoundingly realized and dread-drenched opening sequences in the history

---

[1] Most notably in such interviews as his 2013 discussion with Rob LeFebvre at creativescreenwriting. com, and in the developer's commentary of the game's PS4 release, *The Last of Us Remastered*.

[2] Many critics suggest that linear Triple-A games suffer from a dissonance between story and gameplay. I generally agree, but I believe both that *The Last of Us* is, for the most part, an exception to this rule, and that such a dissonance is not always a bad thing.

[3] *The Last of Us* currently holds a Metacritic rating of 95%.

FIGURE 3.1
The Last of Us **PlayStation 3 Cover Art**

The Last of Us PlayStation 3 cover art.

of the medium" (2013), and he isn't wrong. The roughly 15-minute first taste of Naughty Dog's world is a cocktail of subtly built tension, quiet character moments, and explosive chaos. From a writer's perspective, it's a terrific example of how to reposition audience expectation through a combination of the surprising and familiar.

Firstly, the basics. The game opens with a cutscene—30-something Joel arrives home in the middle of the night to find his daughter, Sarah, asleep on the couch.

> *Joel:* Scoot.
> *Sarah:* Fun day at work, huh?
> *Joel:* What are you still doing up? It's late.
> *Sarah:* Oh, crud. What time is it?
> *Joel:* It's way past your bedtime.
> > *Sarah checks the overhead clock.*
> *Sarah:* But it's still today.
> *Joel:* Honey, please not right now. I do not have the energy for this.
> > *Sarah hands Joel a small box.*
> *Sarah:* Here.
> *Joel:* What's this?
> *Sarah:* Your birthday.
> > *Joel opens the box.*

Sarah: You kept complaining about your broken watch... So I figured, you know. You like it?

    Joel holds the watch to his ear, pretending that it's broken.

Joel: Honey, this is...

Sarah: What?

Joel: It's nice, but I- I think it's stuck. It's not-

Sarah: What? No, no, no, no.

    She sees that he's joking.

Sarah: Oh, ha, ha.

Joel: Where did you get the money for this?

Sarah: (sarcastically) Drugs. I sell hardcore drugs.

Joel: Oh, good. You can start helping out with the mortgage then.

    Sarah laughs.

Sarah: Yeah, you wish.

Meaning here is created through a focus on character and relationships, grounding the player in a world that feels immediately recognizable in spite of how alien it is soon to become. The use of humor suggests a closeness and a history for Joel and Sarah, indicating that I am as much an audience of this story as I am a participant. This is a recurring theme throughout the whole script.

The cutscene continues as Joel carries Sarah up to bed, and in this quiet and familiar moment she is the blonde-haired, blue-eyed incarnation of my own expectant tension, sleeping a little too peacefully in the calm before the storm. I know something bad is likely to happen—Sarah's not on the cover of the game—and when the phone rings and she wakes up and I finally gain her control, it is with a sense of dread and apprehension that becomes embodied, and suddenly very real. I am Will, a 23-year-old male, controlling this pretend 12-year-old girl as she searches for her father in the darkened hallways of their Texas home. "Dad? Daddy? You in here?" I push the left thumb-stick nervously forward; interactivity here is limited, tellingly, to the point-and-gasp dialect of an amusement park—Sarah's pace of movement is locked to a faltering walk, she can explore only a handful of rooms, and the sirens of passing police cars flare, disturbingly, just outside the realm of her current understanding. She's a passive observer, cautiously curious, unable to affect the world in any meaningful way. In contrast to the game's marketed promise of male-directed high-octane action, she is in fact nothing more than an innocent little girl in pyjamas.[4] "Dad? Dad?! What is goin' on?" Critic Alisha Karabinus reflects:

> In that opening, when we are playing as Joel's daughter, when frightening things are happening outside and there are eight missed calls on dad's cell phone – and he is missing – we are Sarah. We don't know anything. We can't do anything but walk around and look out the window and wonder.
>
> *(2013)*

This sense of player-character unity, of *embodiment*, is a unique aspect of video game storytelling. It represents a oneness of game and gamer—text and reader—that is very difficult to achieve, the product of an expertly measured creative recipe in which the sequence's narrative elements are given equal weight to the mechanics of gameplay.[5] The layering of artistic detail, unfolding from Sarah's bedroom into the house and the streets and beyond, and the precise and subtle controls—a slow moving x-axis means you can never be sure what's around the next corner—combine to create meaning that transcends each isolated ingredient: the bright light from Joel's bedroom, the distant barking of a dog, the buzzing of an orphaned cell phone, and the silence and darkness of what is essentially, in the player's mind, a haunted house. We continue on, and I'm learning to navigate the playspace in the same twitched movements of the nervous heroine. "Dad? Daddy? ... Where the heck are you?" Seriously Joel, where the fuck have you gone? With Sarah, I experience both a mechanical *and* a thematic bond, and the result is a form of experiential role-play in which I feel compelled to do the character and her story justice. It makes actually *playing* the game so much more affecting than simply watching it; even in the age of YouTube and Twitch, no game worth its salt can be properly enjoyed without a controller in hand (Figure 3.2).

The sequence evolves when I at last find Joel in his study. In another quick cutscene, he guns down a diseased next-door neighbor. It's my first glimpse of the game's violence, and it's suitably disturbing; Sarah's eyes are wide, her face white with shock. "You shot him... I saw him this mornin'." We head outside as Joel's brother, Tommy, arrives in a truck, and it's from the backseat, my only control a 360° camera through which to glimpse the fleeting terror, that my perspective as this helpless onlooker, this child, is reinforced.

---

[4] Anna Anthropy has lamented that most games are about "men shooting men in the face." While that has probably never been less true than it is now, it's certainly true of *The Last of Us*. But Naughty Dog's game is about more than that, too. In how many Triple-A games do you start by controlling a little girl?

[5] As Brooke Maggs says in Chapter 2, "it's when they [story and gameplay] work together that things work really well."

FIGURE 3.2
Playing as Sarah

Acting, set-design, lighting, and direction—modern games borrow much from film.[6]

We make our way into town, uncertainty creeping in from every direction, and I'm bearing witness in real time to the sudden concentration of humanity down to its most primal force—survival—embodied by a desperate family on the side of the road that Joel forces his brother to disregard. In terms of interactivity, the game has thus far kept me at arm's length, but that's exactly how my character feels too. The result is that I am more powerfully attached to her fate, completely invested in how the rest of the prologue is going to play out (Figure 3.3).

The truck crashes, flips onto its side—we're out in the danger now. It's in this next sequence that I finally gain control of Joel, shielding his daughter from the total riotous chaos of the crumbling street. Sarah's role as my emotional perspective in this early section of the narrative has been clearly established, and it's through the power of interactivity, that notion of embodiment, that this can be achieved so quickly, and it's why the potentially fraught transition from young girl to adult man works so well. I'm Sarah's father now, and yet my brief gameplay time spent in her shoes, working in tandem with the early dialogue and cutscenes, makes me instantly protective. "We're almost there. We're almost there, baby." I guide Joel through hordes of terrified civilians with no other goal, no other thought, than to save his (my, our) daughter. Those elements of the outside world that from the relative safety of Tommy's truck were merely glimpsed—people screaming wildly, crashed cars, police

---

[6]Druckmann has noted specifically that *The Last of Us* was heavily influenced by Alfonso Cuaron's 2006 film, *Children of Men*.

FIGURE 3.3
View from Rear Seat

As the player, you're not always in the driver's seat.

sirens, flames leaping from broken windows—now coalesce in stark and brutal clarity. And my role as the player has met the standard of the scene; at last,
buoyed with a clear purpose—a mission—I'm granted the ability to run.

> *Joel lifts Sarah from the wreckage of the crash.*
> *Joel:* I'm here, baby. I'm here. Come on, gimme your hand.
> > *Sarah stumbles in pain.*
> *Joel:* What is it?
> *Sarah:* My leg hurts.
> *Joel:* How bad?
> *Sarah:* Pretty bad.
> *Tommy:* We're gonna need to run.
> > Joel turns, seeing people fleeing in blind panic.
> *Joel:* Oh my god.
> > *He hands Tommy his pistol.*
> *Joel:* You keep us safe.
> > *He lifts Sarah into his arms.*
> *Joel:* Come on, baby. Now hold on tight.
> *Sarah:* Okay... Daddy, I'm scared.
> > *All around them people are being violently attacked,*
> > *collapsing to the ground, screaming.*
> *Joel:* Keep your eyes closed, honey.
> > *A gas station explodes in a ball of flames.*
> *Sarah:* Oh my- Oh my god...

> *Tommy:* Keep running.
> *Sarah:* Those people are on fire.
> *Joel:* Don't look, Sarah… Keep looking at me, baby.
> > *Tommy spots a way forward.*
> *Tommy:* Over there!
> *Joel:* We're gonna get out of this. I promise.

It is a testament to the game's writing that it is impossible to tell, simply from reading the script, when this cutscene ends and the playable sequence begins. The dialogue remains both context-relevant and thematically consistent, even as I guide Joel frantically onward, twisting the camera like mad in apprehension of what we might see.

The prologue can be viewed as a microcosm of the entire game—what a father will do to protect his child—but it's Naughty Dog's use of perspective, particularly, that stands out as the most relevant feature for a discussion of story-meaning. As well as when to give and withhold interactivity, as in gameplay and cutscenes, respectively, the question for developers of *who* or *what* the player can control is an essential component in the creation of meaning, and this can rest fundamentally on the position of the player as either inside or outside the game world. Some games treat the player as an external, God-like entity, providing a broad set of tools with which he or she can interact.[7] Traditionally, linear games like *The Last of Us*, with a strong focus on story, tend not to acknowledge the player other than in blunt, sometimes unavoidable, ways, such as gameplay tutorials. The player usually inhabits one character at a time, influencing the game world as if from the point of view of an individual within it. As Brooke Maggs notes in our interview in Chapter 2, player perspective is different to character perspective, and the two can be made to align or intersect in myriad ways.[8] Switching from Sarah to Joel affects how the story is told, relocating not only my role as the player, but also my emotions and expectations as a viewer, in relation to the events of the scene.

Toying with perspective is nothing new in storytelling—creative writers have done it for centuries—but when explored through gameplay it can be particularly effective. Video games already borrow from literature a vocabulary of creative shorthand—the concepts of "first" and "third person," for example—and they must continue to use such devices in ways that are unique to the medium. This is all part of Druckmann's "language." Through an attention to many of the traditional tenets of long-form storytelling—coherent

---

[7] Think *Age of Empires* (1997) and *The Sims* (2000).
[8] See Chapter 2.

FIGURE 3.4
Joel and Sarah

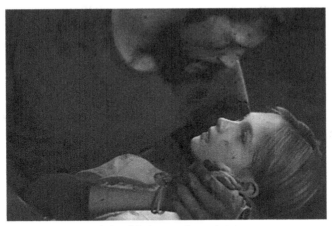

Big moments in cutscenes earn their weight in gameplay, and vice versa.

world-building, consistent character arcs, believable conflict—*The Last of Us* sets a platform upon which its interactive strengths—its gameplay and environmental design—can build.[9]

With Tommy and his gun providing an opportunity to escape, Joel and Sarah flee to the outskirts of the city, and another cutscene plays. There's a man with a walkie-talkie—a soldier—and he's given instructions via radio to open fire. "Sir, there's a little girl… But… Yes, sir." Realizing too late, Joel attempts in vain to shield Sarah from the spray of bullets. She's hit, yelping in agony, and Joel rushes in desperation to her side. "Sarah!" He picks her up, fighting back tears, pleading with her to hold on—"don't do this to me, baby girl"—but she can't. The screen cuts to black, and the opening credits begin to roll. I take a deep breath. Now the game truly begins (Figure 3.4).

Everything Happens for a Reason

The prologue is successful because of how it embraces, rather than resists, many of the traditions of linear storytelling, and yet these same traditions can provide challenges for game design that are fiendishly difficult to overcome. The most

---

[9] Druckmann's "language" is in this way somewhat akin to Walt Williams' analogy of game design as architecture. See Chapter 1.

prominent of these challenges rests at the heart of the author-player struggle—
pacing. Unlike film, in which a director can manage the speed and angle at
which events are revealed, the velocity of a video game narrative depends pre-
dominantly on the person on the couch. Aside from during cutscenes or scripted
gameplay events, the player determines—whether by choice or due to degrees
of proficiency—not the who or the why of the plot (although this is sometimes
the case), but the *when*. The most common result is a fracturing of events that,
at best, makes game narratives feel disjointed, and, at worst, completely disrupts
the flow and consistency essential to the telling of any convincing story. For
this reason, as Walt Williams suggests in Chapter 1, most *gameplay* tends to
boil down to thin variations of anything that doesn't greatly impact plot. In the
action genre (in most genres, actually), this usually means combat; it's rare for
big-budget games to give control to the player unless with the express impera-
tive to mow down a bunch of bad guys. Druckmann himself reflects:

> In some ways, writing a passive medium is freer in that the story can go
> anywhere. You could have a moment that has no physical conflict in it.
> Characters could just sit at a table and talk for fifteen minutes. You can't
> do that in an action game. So everything you're doing, everything you
> set up has to lead to some physical conflict.

(2013)

This philosophy, to prioritize mechanically satisfying gameplay above all else,
is at direct odds with the sort of strict narrative order that makes linear stories
work. The most common "solution," at least in the Triple-A space, is to insert
half-baked interactive moments, such as quick time events or contextual button prompts, into tightly scripted cinematic sequences. These shallow devices
provide little opportunity for failure and are therefore only minimally engaging, and often work to distract rather than absorb the player.[10] The challenge
for linear games is therefore to balance a consistently gratifying gameplay
loop with more heavily directed sequences, without diminishing the effects
of either.[11] It's a challenge *The Last of Us* meets, for the most part, very well;
my only significant criticism of the game is that there is probably too much
combat, especially in later chapters. It's a common problem in Triple-A
games, and it actually alters the effects of gameplay as much as of narrative.
Greater variety in the alignment of gameplay to story would have helped not
only to elevate the major themes of Druckmann's script, but also to heighten

---

[10] I'm generally not a big fan of QTEs in cutscenes. As Walt Williams says in our interview in
Chapter 1, "let me just enjoy what your cinematic team put together."

[11] For a discussion of gameplay loops, see our interview with Brendan Keogh in Chapter 4.

the emotional impact when combat does occur. Firing a gun means a hell of a lot more when you don't get to do it very often.

However, when compared with the mindless bloodletting found in the majority of Triple-A action games, *The Last of Us* exercises admirable restraint. In its opening hours, particularly, the game is more than anything a portrait of character and world. This was a clear focus of Naughty Dog's writing process, from the game's inception all the way through development, and the results are evident throughout. An attention to theme and story-meaning, rather than merely the A to B of pure plot, grounds most of the gameplay in realistic character motivations and reactions, which also works to keep the player emotionally invested.

> What I find interesting…is the characters…what are they trying to say, and ultimately what are you trying to say as a writer through them… This genre has usually been very plot driven instead of character driven… *The Last of Us* is really not about that. It's about a family.
>
> *(Druckmann, 2013)*

With Sarah tragically killed at the end of the prologue, Joel's story picks up 20 years later in a United States ravaged by the spread of a seemingly incurable virus known as Cordyceps. He's living rough, smuggling drugs and weapons in and out of a quarantine zone in Boston with his partner, Tess. Now in his late 40s, Joel is joyless, violent, and gray, with little to live for. The pair strikes a deal with Marlene, the leader of a revolutionary militia group known as the Fireflies, to transport a girl named Ellie to the Capitol Building in exchange for supplies. It is soon revealed that although bitten 3 weeks earlier by one of the so-called "Infected," Ellie has somehow shown no ill signs, and appears, in fact, to be immune. Upon reaching the Capitol Building, where their Firefly counterpart awaits in a pool of his own blood, Tess reveals that she herself has been bitten, and will not survive. She convinces Joel that Ellie represents a genuine chance for a cure, and that he has a responsibility to take her onward. "This is fucking real, Joel. You've got to get this girl to Tommy's." Tess sacrifices herself to give Joel and Ellie time to escape, and the unlikely duo set off together in search of Joel's brother.

Tom Bissell calls *The Last of Us* "proudly and stylishly 'literary'" (2013), and it's in my first few hours alone with Joel and Ellie that this is most apparent. In these early stages I am more fully engaged by the game's "excellent, sensible, and understated" (Bissell, 2013) script than its fairly standard gunplay. This isn't a knock on *The Last of Us* as a *game*; rather, it's a testament to the quality of the writing, and an example of how story can work just as effectively as gameplay as a tool for player investment. Most games throw the player immediately into combat, as if without any faith (often for good reason) in either the story or the game world to hold interest. And yet for killing a bad guy to really mean something, there must first be established a context, and *The Last of Us* is unique because of how deliberately it goes about setting things up. Controlling Joel in these early hours, I revel in simply walking through the game world, slowly learning more about what it means to be on this journey. Naughty Dog use a variety of nontextual tools with which to build their world, and this kind of environmental storytelling, which Eddie explores at length in Chapter 7, is another distinctive form of expression in the language of games. It plays to the strengths of the medium—scrawled graffiti, overheard conversations—revealing itself to the player (or not) in the natural cadence of play, unforced and seemingly unauthored, in a way that other forms of storytelling cannot so comfortably manage.

> There's so much storytelling that happens in the environment, and there's so much storytelling in just the sound effects, or when we don't play sound effects and we just let things be quiet.
>
> *(Druckmann, 2013)*

World-building is a multilayered thing. Strewn throughout the game are collectables—Firefly pendants, comic books, artifacts, training manuals—as well as letters and audio recordings left behind by unseen characters. These additions remain superfluous to the core plot but are there for willing players to seek out as a kind of supplement to in-game events. This is a unique aspect of the strange alternate reality that developers create, making the story of a game feel grounded in a context and history that exists beyond its virtual walls.[12] And these extra narrative bites can prove oddly, unexpectedly satisfying. About a third of the way through the game, during the "Suburbs" chapter,[13] the player can discover a series of notes left behind by a man called Ish. He is never seen in person, or even referenced in dialogue, but snippets of his story unfold in each newly found note, combining to reveal the tragic tale of a very good man. It's subtle and unobtrusive, and immensely effective; Ish was so popular among players that many wondered if his story would comprise the main thrust of the game's downloadable content[14] (DLC)—

---

[12]This idea recalls Damon Reece's discussion of *Metroid Prime*, in Chapter 8.

[13]Like many story-driven games, *The Last of Us* categorises its progression in "chapters" rather than "levels" reflecting a deliberate attention to story.

[14]DLC is additional content for a game, such as extra story missions or multiplayer maps, distributed online by developers after the game's initial release.

another source of additional story-making in video games—which ultimately focused on Ellie instead (Figure 3.5).

While each of these narrative devices serves an important function, the game's beating heart is the evolving relationship between Ellie and Joel. Writing in close partnership with game director Bruce Straley, Druckmann focused on how bearing witness to this relationship would comprise the core experience of playing through *The Last of Us*:

> The two of us were intrigued with doing something where the whole game would be focused on a relationship of two characters, and every decision we make would be helping to form that bond between the two characters.[15] The mechanics it is using, the music choices, the level design and the events that happen in a level, will all help build this bond.

> *(2013)*

FIGURE 3.5
Ish's Note

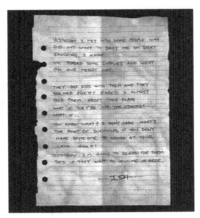

Stories like Ish's add texture to the tone and themes of the game world.

---

[15] This kind of concentrated narrative attention evokes what Brooke Maggs says about *Hellblade: Senua's Sacrifice* in Chapter 2: "having boundaries and restrictions on what you can do in development really makes for a creative game sometimes." The Triple-A industry could benefit greatly from the kind of self-restraint in planning that leads to more tightly focused stories.

This relationship, touched by both tragedy and fleeting triumph, provides brief moments for reflection in which bonds are forged—between Joel and me, Joel and Ellie, Ellie and me, the world and all of us—and personal details revealed. Druckmann notes that "the more time these characters spend with one another, the more they change" (2013), and there is indeed a pure, literary joy in baring witness to this gradual process.

> *After narrowly surviving a highway ambush, Joel and Ellie scavenge for*
> *supplies in a gas station.*
> *Ellie:* How did you know?
> *Joel:* Know what?
> *Ellie:* About the ambush?
> *Joel:* I've been on both sides.
> *Ellie:* Oh. So, ah, you've killed a lot of innocent people?
>   *Joel sighs.*
> *Ellie:* I'll take that as a yes.
> *Joel:* Take it however you want.

Character is exposed through dialogue even outside of cutscenes, forcing shifts in perspective for the characters as well as for me. The pace of these revelations—they come in fragments rather than broad expositional dumps—reinforces the sense that Joel and Ellie are more than mere digital avatars. As time passes, they continue to learn about each other and themselves, and I am there every step of the way to do the same. That these moments are spread across the course of the entire game helps to give Joel and Ellie's journey the sense of a consistent arc.[16] Chris Franklin notes:

> This is a game that knows its most powerful moments aren't explosions
> or gunshots, but quiet moments where a camera lingers too long or a
> painful truth is begrudgingly confronted.
>
> *(2013)*

The passing of time in *The Last of Us* is tuned broadly to the rhythm of the changing seasons, progressing post prologue from the summer of 2033 to spring the next year. This clear demarcation works as an intermediate layer of context within which to frame the central plot against wider events, providing a strong temporal backbone for the narrative's skeleton. Many games have

---

[16] This is one of the game's real strengths. For a discussion of character arcs, see our interview with Brendan Keogh in Chapter 4.

trouble reconciling the colossal scope of bombastic, universe-saving odysseys with the dozen or so real-life hours it takes to complete them, but play time and narrative time in *The Last of Us* feel perfectly aligned. In keeping with its "novelistic" spirit, the game exemplifies an approach to creative writing that appreciates how the give and take of small and large details affects meaning on a range of narrative scales.

> The thing that makes writing this game much easier is that the structure is very episodic. So you can look at each area that they reach in the game as a mini story, its own short story, its own arc.
>
> *(Druckmann, 2013)*

The best example of one of these short stories is Chapter 9, "Lakeside Resort." We're in the dead of winter, having jumped ahead some time from a shoot-out at an abandoned university. With Joel seriously injured, Ellie is forced out on her own to look for supplies. While by this stage of the game she has proven herself to be an extremely capable partner, to find myself controlling her now, all alone on a snowy Colorado mountain, suggests a dramatic shift in tone. It's the second such perspective change in the game, and, as when suddenly switching from controlling to protecting Sarah in the prologue, it works to effectively realign my emotional standpoint both as a player and as an observer. I am now the real-world embodiment of Ellie's clear isolation and vulnerability, which are reinforced symbolically by the harsh realities of winter. While tracking a deer through the snow—a quiet, reflective sequence in blunt juxtaposition to the chaos that precedes it—we meet David, an enigmatic survivor with claims of kinship. "We're from a larger group—women, children—we're all very, very hungry." Like Ellie, I've learned not to trust outsiders—at least, it's no longer my default position—and my bullshit detector at this moment is set to high alert. And for good reason, as it turns out; David is soon revealed to be a cruel and singular threat—possibly a pedophile, almost definitely a cannibal—whose atrocities, with the same deft restraint that is a feature of the game's entire script, are initially hinted at rather than openly displayed (Figure 3.6).

> *Ellie and David seek refuge in a cabin after fighting off waves of Infected.*
> David: You handled yourself pretty nice back there… I say we make a pretty good team.
> Ellie: Psshh. We got lucky.
> David: Lucky? No, no… No such thing as luck. No, you see I believe that everything happens for a reason.

FIGURE 3.6
Winter

The hunter or the hunted? It's rarely as simple as good versus evil.

    Ellie: Sure.

   David: I do. And I can prove it to you. Now, this winter has been especially cruel. A few weeks back, I ah…sent a group of men out—nearby town to look for food. Only a few came back. They said the others had been ah, slaughtered by a crazy man. And get this, he's a crazy man travelling with a little girl. You see? Everything happens for a reason.

The action in this chapter converges with ruthless velocity on a single, dreadful point, as David's true intentions are revealed. He captures Ellie, cages her like an animal,[17] and once again I assume control of Joel. Another perspective change. He wakes up, clearly in immense pain, and it is apparent that for both of us there is only one thing in the world that currently matters: finding Ellie. "Where the hell are you?" This setup marks a return to a classic video game structure—since the days of Mario's earliest adventures, the player has been driven forward by a clear, practical goal—and in the context of this "short story" it provides a defined third act. It also underlines the essential thesis of

---

[17] The image of Ellie devouring food scraps on her hands and knees, locked behind steel bars, vividly mirrors her role at the beginning of the chapter as the hunter. These subtle thematic touches speak to a care and attention to writing that is extremely rare in Triple-A video games.

this chapter: conventional storytelling techniques, when combined with the unique elements of this interactive medium, can be highly useful in creating meaning. What makes this sequence particularly effective is that the goal of the player and character are wholly aligned. As in the prologue, where Sarah and I shared the role of powerless spectator, here Joel and I are similarly united by our desperation to achieve the same outcome.[18] This player-character identity is a major part of Druckmann's "language" of story-driven games, and it is reinforced in this moment by every significant narrative element of the game world: from the worsening blizzard to a rise in gameplay difficulty to the ruthless tone of Joel's dialogue—each aspect of design reflects the fundamental tensions of the story. This may seem like a triumph purely in game design, but it is also an achievement in storytelling. Or, more precisely, it reveals how these apparently divergent creative aspects of Triple-A development, for so long destined to conflict, can in fact be viewed as two sides of the same coin. For without a sense of tension and desperation in the game's narrative, those same textures in gameplay would prove frustrating and out of sync.

This promotion of narrative through every facet of game design—particularly interactivity—is what makes the experience of playing *The Last of Us* work on so many different levels. It's like I'm part-player, part-author, part-audience—every moment is a natural extension of the one before it, and I'm wholly convinced by each character's motivations and reactions. Take the cutscene of Joel interrogating two of David's thugs. He's got them tied up, helpless, and he's demanding to know where they're keeping Ellie. "Focus right here. Right here. Or I'll pop your goddamn knee off." This is Joel at his angriest, most brutal self; a Joel I knew existed but hadn't yet seen. The game doesn't simply produce this moment out of nowhere; it's been earned over hours of character development,[19] previously hinted and suggested, and so when it finally arrives I am right there with it, completely tuned to the key of the narrative as it is now being played. Chris Franklin argues that *The Last of Us* suffers from an "oil and water" (2013) approach to design, where storytelling and gameplay fail to mix, but examples like this one, which is followed almost immediately by Ellie's desperate showdown with her savage captor, reveal how traditional methods of creative writing can combine with shifting mechanics to become the essential ingredient of a game's overall recipe.

---

[18] Both of these examples recall Brooke Maggs' reflections on her favorite recent games.

[19] As Brendan Keogh says, "character progression is just fundamental to basic narrative." But we don't always see it in games.

Franklin's observation represents the most common perspective on the limits of story-heavy video games, and a major point of discussion in this book. The gameplay/cutscene model, however well disguised, faces a clear challenge to achieve a sustained sense of interactive and narrative cohesion. How can a game, with all the complications of interactivity—the presence of a player, the need for challenge and progression, the unavoidable fracturing of narrative pacing—possibly work as a vehicle for coherent, meaningful stories?[20] It's a compelling point, arguably self-evident when considered in the light of most contemporary games. But I don't fully agree. Taking *The Last of Us* as a primary example, the need to work *with* those complications, rather than against them, becomes readily apparent. I'm playing as Joel, hunkering down behind cover, two bullets left in my pistol and another snowstorm blowing in, encircled by watchful baddies whose instructions are to shoot on sight. Here, many hours in, this gameplay setup—in which death is likely and frustration all but guaranteed—fits completely with the narrative. I press onward, learning from my mistakes with every new effort, urging Joel to run a little faster this time, to crouch a little lower, be a little surer of his aim. And I'll be damned if the tension and the dread, the game's "amazing sense of urgency" (Moriarty, 2013), those very tonal tenets to which Duckmann and Straley have pinned their flag, do not in these moments feel heightened, closer than ever before to matching precisely the story of a desperate man on a desperate journey that with my eventual success continues to unfold. The point is that by welcoming those unique aspects of the medium alongside more traditional storytelling techniques, we are able to recognize what once appeared to be problems as possibilities. A player's presence can influence character, gameplay challenge can inform narrative pacing, and the push and pull of authored and emergent meaning can reinforce the tone of a story world (Figure 3.7).

There Is No Other Choice Here

Ellie kills David. It's brutal and horrific, the single most violent moment in the game. Taking Joel and Ellie's relationship as a whole, it marks the point from which neither will truly be able to return, as least not as the people they once were. It's somewhat unusual for a game to continue after the apparent triumph of its protagonists, and defeating David, particularly after such a

---

[20]This point is made, perhaps most famously, by Jonathan Blow in his talk at the 2008 Montreal International Games Summit, "Fundamental Conflict in Contemporary Game Design."

FIGURE 3.7
Joel and Ellie

Balance is a key to meaning in *The Last of Us*.

long and challenging sequence, would appear for Ellie to mark some kind of end. And yet *The Last of Us* it different to most games; it wants us to stay with these characters, to observe how such an event might change them,[21] to reflect in ourselves how the line between good and evil is rarely, if ever, clear. So I continue on, into the game's final stanza, wondering how on earth these two poor souls can keep finding something to fight for.

The ending, ironically, takes place in spring, that eternal symbol of renewal and hope. We're in Salt Lake City, on our way to St Mary's Hospital, where the Fireflies supposedly await. Joel is back to normal, and thankfully, because our path through an underground tunnel turns out to be blocked by a great horde of Infected. This is the most unnecessary segment in the game—combat for the sake of combat—and after the urgent horrors of winter it feels detached and perfunctory, doing more to exasperate than anything else. Most popular fiction tends to finish with a flurry, but video games are especially beholden to the mantra that a bang is always better than a whimper, tending to splurge everything—enemies, puzzles, weapons—in the name of a big, grand finale. The reason for this has more to do, interestingly, with gameplay than with story; as players progress through a game, gaining knowledge and expertise to match the player-character's own steady acquisition of items and skills, there is an obvious need for the stakes and difficulty to rise. An easily won victory is no victory at all.

---

[21] It's similar, if less overt, to *Spec Ops: The Line*, which highlights the effects on its protagonist of his own harrowing journey. See our interviews with Walt Williams and Brendan Keogh in Chapters 1 and 4, respectively.

We get through in one piece, making our way over gushing waters on the side of a tipped-over bus. For everything she has learnt so far, Ellie remains, somewhat comically, unable to swim,[22] and so when Joel falls beneath the surface, frantic with every flailing breath to save her, I know to expect the worst. He drags her to safety, and, in a cutscene that is eerily reminiscent of the tragic end to the prologue, kneels over her unconscious form in pure desperation, as a pair of armed Fireflies approach. "Hands in the air. Hands in the fucking air!" They knock him out with the butt of a gun, and the screen goes black.

He wakes up on a hospital bed, confused; Ellie's gone, and Marlene, the Firefly leader we first met in Boston, explains why.

Marlene: You don't have to worry about her anymore. We'll take care of-
Joel: I worry. Just let me see her, please.
Marlene: You can't. She's being prepped for surgery.
Joel: The hell you mean, surgery?
Marlene: The doctors tell me that the Cordyceps, the growth inside her, has somehow mutated. It's why she's immune. Once they remove it, they'll be able to reverse-engineer a vaccine. A vaccine.
Joel: But it grows all over the brain.
Marlene: It does.
Joel: Find someone else.
Marlene: There is no one else.

Marlene leaves, giving orders for Joel to be shot if he tries to intervene. It all plays out in a cutscene, forcing me into a predetermined narrative predicament from which there is no escape. At this most vital juncture, I have been assertively positioned outside the four walls of the story world. Marlene is right—there is no other choice. That the moral stakes weigh so heavily on this moment only makes it harsher; Joel can either allow the Fireflies to use Ellie for a possible cure—potentially saving humanity—or do whatever it takes to rescue her no matter the human cost. It's the central question of the entire game, a sick conflict ironically presented in a hospital. And I don't get a say in how it goes down, required instead to act on Joel's choice regardless of whether or not it happens to match up with my own. This is a divisive feature in all narrative games, marked frequently as a denial of one of the

---

[22]This is a character trait with direct implications for gameplay. The player is tasked throughout the game with finding wooden palettes to transport Ellie across water in simple environmental puzzles.

fundamental tenets of the medium, and apparently in direct conflict to the events of winter, in which my desperation to rescue Ellie from David was only reinforced by everything the game was asking me to do. But it works here, because the writers have earned it, creating characters with believable motivations and a world with realistic consequences. It is essential for the meaning of this story that the experience, in the terms of pure plot, cannot be changed. Chris Plante surmises:

> If the player has complete control of the story…then the writer has no control… You're a participant in the story, but it is not your story to tell.
>
> *(2013)*

I fight my way through the hospital, taking out Marlene's men with Terminator-like efficiency. Joel has become a killing machine, willing to do whatever necessary to get what he wants. Adam Sessler calls the game's violence "intimate and unsettling," but "totally consistent with the tone established throughout" (2013), and this marriage of content and form achieves its zenith in these final moments of combat. Reduced to his most essential self, driven solely by his desire to save Ellie, Joel now embodies the inhuman purity of the Infected—he *is* the last of us.

We reach Ellie moments before the surgery begins; she's unconscious, lying prone under bright operating lights, flanked by three surgeons, and as incapable as I am to stop Joel from doing what he has decided needs to be done. I move into the room—two of the surgeons back away, nervous, but one of them picks up a scalpel. "I won't let you take her. This is our future. Think of all the lives we'll save." It's the most important moment in the game, encapsulating perfectly the tension between gameplay and story that is at the heart of how interactive narratives can fail or flourish. Convention suggests that Rule Number One of game design is to *empower* the player, to put me in the driver's seat in every facet of the experience.[23] This is, primarily, a gameplay directive; its influences on story tend to come as a natural consequence—a game's narrative and world are made to fit the structure of its gameplay. The alternative to this convention, refreshingly employed in *The Last of Us*, is for the player-character to be realistically fragile, emotionally and physical *human*, and for his interactions with the game world to naturally reflect this. This is achieved through a focus—tradition in most media, but wholly refreshing in games—on the second part of that moniker: *character*. By promoting the otherness of its protagonist as totally unequivocal—and this works especially well

---

[23] Walt Williams reflects on the problems surrounding player agency and empowerment in Chapter 1.

in third-person games in which the player-character is physically rendered and visible at all times—Naughty Dog treads more complex thematic ground, and not at the expense of gameplay. Even if I don't agree with his choices, stepping into Joel's shoes becomes an exercise in role-play, a deeply enriching experience that heightens the emotional connection between player and character by highlighting the fact that we are distinct and separate entities.

> We are the game's pistol; we are the game's lead pipe; we are the game's smoke bombs and its bow and arrows. But no matter how much we might want to pretend otherwise, we are not this game's characters.
>
> *(Franklin, 2013)*

And we should embrace that fact. In its explicit denial of my agency, *The Last of Us* reinforces the thesis that proudly authorial—even *literary*—game stories are not only possible, but can actually turn their perceived limitations into avenues for creating meaning. As the believable, perhaps inevitable, result of everything that has come before it, the sequence works as a piece of interactive storytelling whether or not the player is on Joel's side. Reviewer Danielle Riendeau recalls:

> I was literally yelling at the screen while playing. I wanted to save the world. I wanted Joel to stop killing everyone who was *trying* to save the world and find some compromise. I really wanted to save Ellie and simply threaten the doctor at the end, who was clearly no physical threat to me. To yell, 'You can have a blood sample, but you can't have the girl!' But I'm so, so happy that the game didn't let me.
>
> *(2013)*

This careful management of interactivity—of what the player can do, and when—should be considered just another tool, albeit an extremely powerful one, in the game designer's repertoire. Neither cutscenes nor gameplay can ever exist without context; they generate meaning in how they interrelate. If story and gameplay are in this way aligned, flowing through every vein of the creative process, working to a shared outcome, then both facets of the game will always be better served (Figure 3.8).

Full disclosure: the first time I played the game, I mowed down those doctors without so much as a second thought. With a flamethrower! It didn't even occur to me to bargain with them, to halt my progress and attempt to find some compromise. In that moment, after all that has happened in the game—"after everything we've been through," as Ellie says—I was going to save her no matter the cost. To me, it made perfect sense. Indeed, it is Naughty Dog's subtle development of character across the course of the entire game that encourages

FIGURE 3.8
Surgery

Choices aren't always what they seem.

the same kinds of change in the player.[24] That this development is sustained coherently for more than a dozen hours is very rare; it's a common experience for me to forget in most games why I'm doing anything. Druckmann and Straley avoid this by utilizing narrative devices that promote story from the top down—dialogue is used to reveal a character's internal world, not just a set of motivations, and so character change can be measured convincingly by how those internal worlds transform in the face of external events. Whereas so many games feel like a mash-up of barely related strands—levels, stages, main missions, side quests—*The Last of Us* is a true sum of its parts.

That notion, of meaning arising from a holistic approach to narrative, is made explicit as Joel saves Ellie. He lifts her from the operating table, whispering, "come on, baby girl. I gotcha…"—that same parental epithet he used to use for Sarah. And when he carries her away through the hospital halls, pursued by the relentless Fireflies, it is that very image from the prologue—his daughter in his arms on a ravaged Texas street—that is most vividly recalled. Naughty Dog knows that story is all about balance—every moment needs to be weighed in the context of every other—and the use of devices such as self-reference and foreshadowing represents a step forward in both the breadth and depth of the vocabulary of video game storytelling (Figure 3.9).

[24]Mark Villamor, at venturebeat.com, captures the feelings of so many players: "as she [Ellie] became the most important thing to Joel, she also became the most important thing to me" (2013).

FIGURE 3.9
Joel Carrying Ellie/Joel Carrying Sarah

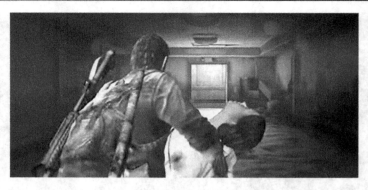

A good story knows itself back to front.

The use of another such device, juxtaposition, is reinforced most powerfully in the game's very final sequence. It begins with a cutscene. We're driving, post hospital-rescue, back to Tommy's farm in Jackson. Ellie finally wakes up, all bleary-eyed, and asks Joel just exactly what went down back there.

> *Joel:* We found the Fireflies. Turns out there's a whole lot more like you, Ellie. People that are immune. It's dozens, actually. Ain't done a damn bit of good, either. They've actually st- .They've stopped looking for a cure. I'm taking us home. I'm sorry.

It's a harrowing instance of dramatic irony. Whereas at the very beginning of the game, Joel was unable, through no fault of his own, to save his daughter, now he is unwilling, to the point of risking the very future of civilization, to let Ellie go. Only now, after all this time, does he have the capacity, the freedom, to make that choice. And that's just it—it's *his* choice, not mine. I sit there, watching on, completely understanding and yet somehow not quite believing what Joel has done. It's a final, stubborn refusal to acknowledge my real-life morality, made especially poignant by what comes next. The cutscene ends as they abandon the ruined car, and this time I'm given control of Ellie as we make our way through the woods on foot. The sun streams in thin shafts through the tall, gently waving trees, and I know there must only be moments left. It's interesting, this final change in player perspective—it lasts barely a minute, but to feel Ellie's presence through my controller is a powerful reminder of what Joel (and I) have been fighting for. And it's plenty of time to make what happens in the final cutscene, triggered as Joel hauls Ellie up the side of the ledge, Tommy's property spread down in the valley below, such a startling and effective ending to the game (Figure 3.10).

It Can't Be for Nothing

There is another moment, before the lying and the interrupted surgery, that perfectly captures the point of this whole darn thing. It's on the way to the hospital, so close to the end of the journey, without an enemy in sight—the calm before the final tempestuous storm. While Joel is fully recovered from his winter injuries, talking idly about playing the guitar, Ellie is distracted, apparently bearing emotional scars that will take far longer to heal. She's barely listening, lagging behind in a cloud of her own thoughts. Where most games clearly pigeonhole their individual components—combat goes here, story goes there—*The Last of Us* reveals how storytelling in games needs to pay attention to how all the parts intersect. The result is moments like this, in which Ellie's mental state realistically recalls previous events. Like Joel, I can see that something is wrong, and I care.

We take a short cut through a bus terminal, and Joel spots the end of a ladder high up on a ledge. After 15 hours of play, I am fluent in the language of this game. I know exactly what's about to happen—I'll boost Ellie up onto the ledge, she'll drop the ladder down for Joel, and we'll continue on our way. We've done it so many times before.

> *Joel:* Everything all right?
> *Ellie:* Yeah, I'm fine.

FIGURE 3.10
Ellie CU

Sometimes it's about what's left unsaid.

Joel: You just kinda seem extra quiet today.
Ellie: Oh, sorry.
Joel: No, it's not...it's fine.
    He sees the ladder.
Joel: Well, we could use that ladder. Here we go.
    He crouches down to boost Ellie up onto the ledge, but she's
    sitting down on a bench, distracted.
Joel: Ellie. Ellie.
Ellie: What?
Joel: The ladder, c'mon.
Ellie: Right... Okay...

But this time it's different. When Ellie gets to the top of the ledge, she sees something, some other distraction, and drops the ladder down before running away out of sight. I hurriedly maneuver Joel up after her, curious and concerned about what might be lying ahead. But she's gone. "Oh...you gotta see this." After chasing her through rooms and along corridors and down stairs, with no idea what we're about to find, I at last catch a glimpse of why she's so excited, and it's not what I expected at all.

It's a giraffe. In the midst of this dark and violent voyage, one that has cost its characters so much, finally a moment of pure light. Joel approaches slowly, reaching out a hand for the animal as it munches on some leaves. "It's alright. C'mere, c'mere." And Ellie, whose entire life has been devoid of anything resembling this kind of natural beauty, can finally allow herself a moment to be distracted by something good. "So fucking cool." We simply watch as, down in a field below, a whole herd of giraffes wanders by—nature has reclaimed this land as its own.

> *Joel:* We don't have to do this. You know that, right?
> *Ellie:* What's the other option?
> *Joel:* Go back to Tommy's. Just…be done with this whole damn thing.
> *Ellie:* After all we've been through. Everything that I've done. It can't be for nothing.

It seems clear to me that the limitations of the Triple-A linear single-player game have been vastly overstated, and this short sequence demonstrates how versatile the language of such experiences can be. By reconfiguring a commonly used mechanic—climbing a ladder—the scene's meaning is altered through interactivity more effectively than by dialogue or visual design alone. When aligned for the same purpose, these seemingly distinct facets of the creative process can elevate a narrative beyond the single possibilities of any one of them. In all creative languages there is room for experimentation and change, and the truth is that a perceived weakness—narrative pacing, challenge as an obstacle to progression—can, in the right hands, be turned into a strength. It's an attitude that fills me, as a gamer and a writer, with tremendous excitement for the future (Figure 3.11).

The goal of this analysis was to show how writing in *The Last of Us* combines with other elements of game design to influence meaning across the board. Ultimately, the game's clear success in this area can be best captured in a quote from Neil Druckmann himself:

> I really believe *The Last of Us*, unless you really change the story, wouldn't be as strong in any other medium.
>
> *(2013)*

That alignment of content and form is a direct result of a studio intent on upholding the sorts of classic dramatic principles that are too often neglected

**FIGURE 3.11
Giraffe**

On a well-worn path, *The Last of Us* finds new places to go.

in Triple-A single-player campaigns—there is a clear narrative arc in which the characters develop and change while remaining grounded in a world whose themes and tone remain consistent throughout.[25] I can't count how many games I've played where the basic purpose of the story is forgotten within minutes in favor of more enemies, bigger guns, and the mindless marshland of impenetrable world lore. Naughty Dog know exactly the story they want to tell, and waste barely a moment in telling it.

And that is perhaps the game's biggest lesson: to have a language, as Druckmann might say, that you know perfectly—every letter, word, and grammatical rule—and to start within its boundaries, slowly stretching them where you can, feeling out for where they might be overcome. After all, no language exists in a vacuum; video game storytelling has and will continue to evolve, and it's how this process develops that is most captivating. *The Last of Us* demonstrates how writers in this medium can employ new and old tools alike in constructing meaningful, enriching narratives.

---

[25] Keeping things "grounded" was almost a mantra for Naughty Dog during development. It's even the title of their behind-the-scenes documentary, *Grounded: The Making of The Last of Us* (2013).

4

Interview with Brendan Keogh

Brendan Keogh is a critic, journalist, and academic based in Brisbane, Australia. He has written about video games for a range of international outlets, including *Polygon*, *Kotaku*, and *Ars Technica*. He is the author of two books, *A Play of Bodies: How We Perceive Videogames* (2018) and *Killing is Harmless: A Critical Reading of Spec Ops: The Line* (2012). He is currently a research fellow in the Digital Media Research Centre at Queensland University of Technology.

Brendan advocates a holistic approach to game design and suggests that writing in games is one small part of a very complex system. We ask him how that system manifests in the best kind of narrative games, and he points to the recent *Wolfenstein* reboots as an example of "sincere" storytelling. However, he believes that the independent scene is a greater source of innovation in video game writing today and encourages everyone to explore the unique stories and techniques of lesser known creators. He suggests that writing in the Triple-A industry is severely limited by convention and expectation, highlighting thematic tensions in *BioShock: Infinite* and *The Last of Us*, and argues that if change is going to come, it will be from outside the traditional space. Brendan wants designers and writers to focus on the total play experience, regardless of technology or platform, and to explore a wider range of genres and narrative methods. Only then, he suggests, can coherent, meaningful storytelling be achieved.

Will Cordner: Let's start with *Killing is Harmless*, a digital novel you wrote in 2012 about *Spec Ops: The Line*. You're interested in violence in games, and its effects on storytelling; one of the things you wrote about was a second wave of shooters coming through, games that interrogate the shooter genre itself.

Now that we're 6 years post-*Spec Ops*, do you believe that this second wave of shooters has in fact come to pass?

Brendan Keogh: There have definitely been other shooters since *Spec Ops* that also engage consciously with those conventions. The *Wolfenstein* franchise [rebooted by Bethesda in 2014 with *A New Order*] stands out as one example. I think there have been repeated first steps since then, but not necessarily a second step. A second step would be something that either wouldn't be a shooter at all, or you would actually start to resolve some of the tensions that *Spec Ops* points at, rather than continuing to simply point at those tensions. Since I wrote *Killing is Harmless*, I've actually started speaking to developers a lot more. I even spoke to some developers from Yager Development. A lot of their really clever critiques in that game came from them being sick of having to make a game like that. They were told to make a military shooter, they were sick of making military shooters, so they made a game that was also sick of military shooters. There has been a lot of that happening in the games industry from 2012 onward—30-something game developers who are sick of making these games, so they're critiquing the genre and the industry while they make them.

TW: I'd be interested to hear more about the *Wolfenstein* series as it relates to that idea. Do you think it's a reflexive look at the shooter, or is it more of an indulgence?

BK: It is an indulgence but it's the right kind of indulgence. Something I've always said about Triple-A games for me is that my favorites are the ones that feel sincere, in that they don't feel like they are trying to be smarter than they actually are. The main reason players are playing shooters is because it's fun to shoot a bunch of stuff. For this reason, I take issue with some shooters, like, for example, *BioShock: Infinite*. I feel it's doing this whole performance of how smart, intellectual, and literary it is but you're really just playing it to shoot things. Whereas a game like *Wolfenstein* has sincerity—it knows what it is and it's not pretending to be anything else. It actually has interesting, well-rounded characters; it has some weird moral tensions, and these amazing, weird, actually quite nuanced monologues from Jimi Hendrix comparing racism in America to Nazism in Germany. It does all that while not pretending that you're playing for a reason other than to shoot a bunch of Nazis. *Wolfenstein II: The New Colossus* (2017) worked really well because it tapped into a current zeitgeist with the rise of the alt-right, the resurgence of white supremacy and the election of Donald Trump. On inauguration day, everyone was loving this meme of a Nazi getting punched in the face, and then you've got this video game that comes along with the cathartic encouragement of, "take out your anger on these Nazis by shooting a bunch of Nazis." *Wolfenstein* is not like *Spec Ops* because it's not reflexive, it's not a shooter about shooters necessarily, but it is thinking about what can be done with the genre and what meanings can be conveyed within the genre.

WC: Reflexive narratives have been fairly common in recent years. How else might story-driven games create meaning, other than just holding a mirror up to themselves? Could there be a shooter in the future that takes itself very seriously but also does more than just poke and prod and interrogate itself?

BK: If we're talking about shooters, then so long as the base game is about staring down a gun and blasting a bunch of targets in corridors, then there's only so much you can do with that in terms of narrative expression. We're seeing Triple-A games and shooters like *Wolfenstein* now start to lean into their genre and are no longer trying to prove something. Whereas I think there were a lot of Triple-A games, especially from 2007 to 2010, which were trying to prove how smart they were and were just like "screw you Roger Ebert, games are art, look at our themes!" Unfortunately, you can't really do any of that within that genre necessarily because that genre is about having fun shooting stuff, and so *Wolfenstein* embraces that. The Triple-A space is not where the powerful and expressive narrative innovations in video games are actually happening. The large commercial blockbuster industry is solely interested in making the action movie equivalent of video games. They're not interested in making the rom-com equivalent or the drama equivalent, and they're not interested in all the genres that aren't action. Where that stuff is happening is indie developers, hobbyists, and amateurs. Studio models that are top-down, large publisher, 200 people making one game have to be very conservative and can't take risks. It's a model that is very hamstrung in terms of what stories it can tell and what innovations with narrative it can make.

WC: Why do you think that is? Does the Triple-A space present too many obstacles for that kind of "auteur" role?

BK: There are a lot of issues with auteur theory and video games. This idea that Hideo Kojima made *Metal Gear Solid* or that Ken Levine made *BioShock* is just wrong. All video games are immensely collaborative, and video game development is an immensely collaborative process across so many different disciplines. You need visual assets, you need audio assets, you need programming, you need design, and you need writing. I've started using the analogy of house building. House building isn't any one discipline; there are concreters, carpenters, architects, electricians, among many others. The idea that any one person can have control over all of that, especially in the Triple-A space, doesn't stand up. Within that ecology, the writer is in a very strange, sidelined position. Every second talk about narrative at the Game Developers Conference each year says, "you have to include writers earlier in the process." Except, if your audience doesn't actually care about story and just wants some basic context to shoot a bunch of guys, then it doesn't actually matter when the writer comes in. On the other hand, if you're trying to tell a deep expressive story experience, then there needs to be a deep and intimate relationship with the writer from the start. Of course, this is very difficult to achieve in a Triple-A space because the game might be being made in three different countries or across an entire EA campus.

WC: I think you make a really important point that often gets overlooked—many people who play Triple-A games don't really care about story. You suggest in your "Notes on *The Last of Us*" that the gameplay gets in the way of the storytelling and world-building. It's funny—I know some people who say it's the other way around. They just want to shoot zombies and kill dudes and they're not really interested in the narrative. Do you think the average gamer cares much about being told a compelling story?

BK: *The Last of Us* really exemplifies a lot of tensions there because it's a very conventional Triple-A game that tried to walk as far away from what conventional Triple-A games are allowed to do as possible, without destroying itself. You have these long moments of quiet where you have only three bullets in the chamber, juxtaposed against walking past all this neat thigh-high cover and knowing you'll be coming back through here to shoot a bunch of dudes. It's really walking this line where it's this game that's really at odds with itself to have its cake and eat it too. There are a lot of video game players out there who do just want action or rather, maybe more fairly, they do not play video games for story. That's for a number of reasons. A lot of research going back to the mid-1980s suggests the games industry as well as games journalism and marketing very deliberately cultivated a certain video game playing audience. This very specific demographic, which took on the name "gamer," was young and male. When the industry started marketing toward this audience, a large focus was placed on this idea of "gameplay," a word that also emerged at this time. This cultivated the idea that real gamers play games for gameplay not for narrative, or graphics, or the audio-visual representational veneer. Real gamers care about mechanics, systems, challenge, and being really good—they're not there to read pages of text. This can be seen in early games studies a lot as well, the idea that video games are held back by narrative and are trying too hard to imitate other storytelling mediums like film, television, or literature. At the same time, I think it's important to realize that narrative is not all video games do, and not all video game experience can be boiled down to a narrative experience. There are a lot of ways that video games mean and express themselves that isn't narrative. The issue *The Last of Us* and a lot of other big games had was that their audiences are so cultivated and hegemonic that they really struggle with a video game that isn't fitting what they expect, and it's very hard to communicate that the game is anything else.

TW: You seem to be advocating an approach that considers the entirety of the game and the play experience. Story and gameplay shouldn't be treated in isolation. It's a sentiment you express in *Across Worlds and Bodies*, too.

BK: Essentially, yes. The journal article you're referring to is the first chapter of my PHD/recent book from early 2018. I would argue that narrative is very important, but it's just another aspect next to mechanics, audio design, visual design, and esthetic. All of these things together become the video game text in terms of a textual experience of play. I would say narrative is just another aspect of the broader game experience.

WC: How hard is it then to isolate those different aspects? You suggest in *Killing is Harmless* that *Spec Ops* is "superbly written." Do you think it's possible to divorce a game's writing from those other creative elements that are so important? In the same way that a terrible game can have amazing graphics, how important is writing, specifically, and what are some other examples of really well-written games you can think of?

BK: It is really important, in which narrative design and in fact all aspects of design work best when they are invisible, which also just means it's hard to actually identify good examples of it, and very easy to identify bad examples. Sorry, I got stuck when you mentioned the fact that I called *Spec Ops* "superbly written." I'm trying to figure out what I meant by that.

WC: Well, one important thing, I think—you mention that the characters and themes "slowly evolve over the course of the entire game." That idea of a clear arc and real character development—these kinds of things are pretty basic in other forms of storytelling. They're essential to coherent, meaningful stories.

BK: The main thing that fascinated me about *Spec Ops,* which I think very few video games are able to do, is exactly that—actually having a narrative arc. Being able to start in one place and end in another place with your character being a radically different person than they were at the start. That character progression is just fundamental to basic narrative. There are very, very few video games where your character is in any way different at the end to how they were at the start beyond narratively meaningless ways such as being Level 50 instead of Level 2. In terms of emotional identity, I can't think of many other games where the character is actually a different person and has actually been impacted in a significant way by what they've gone through. When I said *Spec Ops* is well written what I meant was that it follows the arc of an actual story. With a lot of Triple-A video games, people will say, "oh, this game's story is amazing," but if that story was reproduced as a book would we be saying that about this 101 "war is bad" narrative, or are we excited that this is a good story…for a video game?

WC: You mentioned before that one of the things that keeps coming up in a lot of this discourse is the writer coming in too late in the development process. That seems to me a real problem if we're talking about these basic and fundamental aspects of storytelling. Do you think it's possible to have something like a consistent narrative arc without having the writer there from the beginning?

BK: It's harder to bring a writer in later and have thematic consistency throughout the whole game. *Spec Ops*, again, was one of those games. One of the things it did really well was that it was not just a good story while you were shooting things; the entire experience felt thematically cohesive. The messiness and choppiness of the shooting, the music, the changing character model of Walker throughout the game—all of it worked together as this broader thematic gravitas about what the game was trying to say. In opposition, one of the negative aspects of *Wolfenstein II: The New Order* is that when I went back and tried to do some writing on it about how great the story was, I realized I was only writing about the cutscenes. You can watch a supercut on YouTube and get all the thematic significance out of it. *Spec Ops* achieved good writing because at every point I felt like I was contributing or resonating with this thematic aspect of the game. That gets harder and harder to do once you have more and more people involved in development. As I said before, even just the base physicality of all the animators are two rooms or two countries over, working on aspects of the game that you don't have direct control over. Triple-A game development is so piecemeal, and there are so many chefs and so many pies. It's difficult. As teams get smaller and as you go to that indie end of the spectrum, down to one person—like Anna Anthropy making *Dys4ia*—you instead get efficient, directed, 5-min-long games about a specific story. Triple-A has so many different people and so many different objectives that thematic consistency is always going to be a challenge, no matter how soon you bring the writer on.

WC: It's that thematic consistency that makes such a difference. You've mentioned the times in games where the themes, the storytelling, and the gameplay all come together—moments when the storytelling is dynamic and emergent, where the story and mechanics combine. Those moments are so rare, but they're also my favorite thing about narrative-driven games. Why are those moments so hard to create? Is it because we're still held back by "gamey" conventions? Or are those moments only possible at the end of a long arc where you've really got to earn them?

BK: I think it's both. You're talking about getting into the "flow" of the game, and that got me thinking about the final level of *Max Payne 3*. It's an incredibly good, goose-bumps-down-your-arm moment. Even though it's just running down a hallway shooting some stuff, it feels as if everything has come to this moment; there is an amazing conclusive narrative gravitas to that play sequence. It's incredibly good, and I think one power large Triple-A developers do have is that all that gamey stuff gets you invested for 5, 10, 20 hours. It's a very basic narrative conceit, because suddenly you're invested in all of this—physically invested from the amount the time you've committed to this stupid video game. So of course you're into what it's doing right there when the camera shifts a little bit and you're controlling another character, or they just kill somebody, or they play a song while you do what you've been doing this whole time. Video games foster an amazing attachment because they require so much labor and so much time. Triple-A has this issue with gaming conventions that it can't easily do away with; they're investing millions and millions of dollars into these games and they need to make a return on these commercial products, which means being attractive to a particular audience that are looking for entertainment that will entertain them for a certain number of hours.

EP: You're talking about the aspect of duration and investing a lot of time, but there also seems to be in these moments a kind of coming together of kinetic learning with a narrative learning. And within that you've got a particular gameplay experience. How do imagine the possibilities of writing that kinetic experience? Is that part of something you can think about as a creative writing aspect? Or is it purely coming from gameplay, and the writing is kind of tacked on?

BK: That's a tricky one. The kinetic aspect is superimportant, and it gets explored a lot through "game feel." I'm going to be a jerk and answer with a question. You refer to "gameplay." What is that? What is gameplay?

WC: That's really an important point; it's something we're attempting to grasp at with this book. I think that in a good game it's much harder to divorce all those aspects from each other. I think for me gameplay can be many things. It's more than just a repeated primary mechanic. It can come through in the environment, or the down time, or even sometimes in what you're not doing. Gameplay can just be hearing an NPC crack-wise while you're walking through the forest—anything that feeds into the overall active experience of playing the game. If we take *The Last of Us* as an example, gameplay there is definitely more than just crouching behind cover and shooting guys in the face.

BK: Totally. I think you're right in that it's a lot harder to look at video games, especially Triple-A video games, holistically—as a single experience. That partly goes back to how they've been developed, but also how we've learnt to comprehend Triple-A video games over the years. Game reviews often review the graphics, the audio, and the gameplay as separate things. The word "gameplay" came from game culture in the late 1980s and early 1990s—a culture of gamers who again are overwhelmingly young men and overwhelmingly care about system-driven, mechanically challenging games. Lots of people use it very generally. They say "gameplay," and it's a useful term in general conversation—a conversation at the pub kind of way. When we talk about the gameplay aspects and the narrative aspects, gameplay has always really, since it was created, been set up as an antagonism against the narrative, representational, textural aspects of video games. I always try never to use the word "gameplay" because I find I have something more interesting to say about video games by not using it. In my work, I suggest that the textural aspect of games is just that—the kinesthetic, kinetic, what it feels like in the hands, the rhythm, the flow, the haptic, and audio-visual and sensory stuff. It all merges together, and narrative context is superimportant there in terms of ensuring it feels right. In some ways, video games are like food; when people say they just want a fun video game, that's essentially saying you want yum food. You want food that tastes good; you want games that feel good. That final level of *Max Payne 3* feels good. Walking along slowly in the snow with Ellie in *The Last of Us* feels good—it's a different good but it's good. *Wolfenstein* feels good when you're rolling around a wheelchair in a submarine shooting Nazis. *Super Meat Boy* feels good primarily in a way that is entirely detached from anything to do with narrative. Really, the primary reason we play games is because they feel good, and they feel good in a way that what we do with our bodies relates to what we're looking at and getting audio-visual feedback from. So as a writer, how you engage with that, well, fundamentally I don't really know—but I think it's primarily about understanding that at their core people play video games because they want to feel a certain way. It's a very carnal engagement as opposed to an intellectual one. There's a bit of mind-body dualism there, but you feel video games in your body, and all the intellectual stuff is in service to that feeling. The hypothetical writer of *Max Payne 3*, on that final level, was hopefully thinking about more than just the discrete narrative arc, but also thinking about what music would be playing, how long it would go for, about whether or not bullets should do less damage so as not to disturb the rhythm of the level. The writer needs to think about the video game holistically.

TW: And so that holistic approach is in service of the player? If the play experience is a broader combination of those things you've mentioned—the physical, the audio-visual, the rhythm—then the design philosophy needs to prioritize a player-centric approach. Is that right?

BK: In my writing, I recommend a player-centric and video game-centric approach, so in that sense, decentering both the player and the video game. This is what I get at in my own book—the text that the critic needs to understand is the player coupled with the video game, which means essentially paying attention to both sides of the screen at once; both what's happening in the video game and what's happening around the video game, and that includes what buttons you're pressing to perform what action, as well as how the UI is designed and how the menus feel to navigate, when is the controller vibrating, when is it not, etc. All that stuff. As the *Metal Gear Solid* person in the room, you'd know well how amusing it is that people like to mock those games and mock Hideo Kojima for essentially wanting to make films. Kojima is making the most video-gamey video games possible in that he is actually fully comprehending the holistic nature of video games. He plays with the audio-visuality of that by, for example, messing with your TV when you're fighting Psycho Mantis. Kojima understands that this is a thing people do on a television set. Or this a thing people do with controllers. The way he integrates both sides of the screen beyond just a fourth wall joke really gets to something fundamental about the video game as an art form.

TW: Yes, I think it does. Speaking of that Psycho Mantis boss fight—it's always been one of the most referenced boss battles in history. It's one that always gets a nod in these kinds of discussions. Could you speak a little to its potency as a play experience?

BK: It's how it speaks to the limitations and liminality of immersion as the desired effect of video games. We think we want to be fully immersed in this world that we want to be Neo stepping into the Matrix—a fully immersive, frameless, "forget your real body, step into this virtual world," experience. We think the best video games do that, but in fact we're always just looking at a television set, or wearing a VR headset, or staring at our phone on the bus. This idea of full immersion doesn't exist. We never leave our situated body behind when we play a video game. What that boss fight does incredibly well is you get the content of the game referring to the form of the game. Players experience a flickering of attention between looking at a flat screen, at UI elements, at menus and HUDs, at the triangles moving around quickly to simulate a three-dimensional world, and then actually feeling like they're in a three-dimensional world. That flickering of attention as a player is explicitly highlighted when a character states, "hello Solid Snake, put the controller down." Players are thinking, "what? That doesn't make sense." But it does make sense. What's amazing about it is that it's not weird; it's just entirely natural that a virtual character can refer to actual elements of video game play. There is a really intimate fusing of actual and virtual aspects of video game play that is irresolvable and which that boss fight draws attention to very nicely.

TW: How should a writer think about those things when designing stories for games? What are some of the best ways to keep that consideration of the player front and center?

BK: One of the main issues game studies have is the idea that what's special about video games is that the player is in charge or that the player decides on what the story will be. But we've been chasing this burning bush of interactivity that's called us into the desert, and now we've just been wondering around for decades. This idea that the ideal video game would be one in which a player tells their own story, where they can make any choice possible and anything possible could happen, is just simply never actually going to be a thing, because making that is impossible. In actual fact, nobody wants that because that's just living, and when we want a story, we want to be *told* a story. Early game studies and popular discourse on game development suggests that the developers should step aside and let the players decide what the game is about. That kind of fell apart gloriously around when *BioShock: Infinite* (2013) came out, and more recently, people have become fed up with centrist positions on topics. If you released a game that was like, "are the Nazis bad or not? You decide," that would not be an appropriate video game to release. Yet that's essentially what *BioShock: Infinite* was about. At some point, there needs to be an author that says, "this is what this is about." But "interactivity" is another word I like to avoid. I like to think of video games as *participatory*. Again, that's very semantic, but I'm trying to get away from those connotations and instead insist that the player isn't in charge of the video game, the player isn't deciding what happens. The player is participating with the video game to allow the text to happen. The player plays with the text, or plays with the work to create the text, and is a fundamental aspect of the textuality in this player-video game hybrid—but they're not the center, they're not the main part. When the video game writer creates a video game experience, they need to be considering the video game as player and video game, not just video game.

They need to be thinking about how the player works as an element of that text.

WC: It seems that the most common way for designers to create a connection there, between player and game, is through mechanics. A core, repeatable gameplay loop, or a set of loops, helps to ground the player within a clearly defined context. And in the Triple-A space, that context is usually one of violence. Do you think we'll ever see big budget, story-driven games that are built upon neither violence nor a limited set of mechanical loops?

BK: No. I can't imagine a Triple-A video game that doesn't revolve around a core mechanical loop because if you don't have a core mechanical loop you instead just have a lot of content to make. That is just a massive waste of resources as far as any commercial undertaking to make a video game would be concerned. It would be like trying to make a film where every scene has different actors. Yes, you *could* do that, but for 99% of films, that's not a valuable use of resources. Even more so for video games, where so many resources go into creating the driving system or the shooting system or whatever. Having to create more systems would just not be valuable.

WC: And would it also perhaps alienate the player? Is that mechanical context important to keep a player's role in the game defined? You potentially lose that when you strip away a core gameplay structure.

BK: Yes. I think the best example of a game like what you're describing is the work of David Cage with Quantic Dream: games like *Fahrenheit, Heavy Rain, Detroit: Become Human*. Those games are games that don't have core loops really, just context-specific button pressing. People expect core loops, and core loops are the reason why people are playing these games. What we are seeing is more video games with downtime and more designers experimenting with downtime. Naughty Dog has been really important for that; they've created games where you can have a 50-min section of walking and talking, and that is fun. Of course, what really deserves credit for that is the whole genre of walking simulators, an entire genre emerged really from *Dear Esther, Proteus*, and *Gone Home*. We've definitely seen that bleed back into Triple-A, and more games now have walking simulator levels. The best example of that would be *Alien: Isolation*, which commits to this survival-horror trope without just giving you waves of enemies to fight. It actually breaks down a lot of gamey conventions in a lot of interesting ways. There are more examples of games like that, but I don't think the entirety of the Triple-A space is going to go that way anytime soon. I don't think Triple-A really has any reason to stop doing what it's doing. What it's doing still makes young male gamers the primary audience Triple-A is interested in, and there will always be more young male gamers.

WC: It's hard to argue with that. Given that sequels, remakes, and reboots are such a big part of popular entertainment, maybe the Triple-A space just isn't where we should be looking for new and interesting storytelling in games. Would you encourage us to expand our gaming horizons?

BK: Yes. I said to my partner yesterday as she was watching the fourth Jason Bourne film, "there are no conclusions under capitalism." There will always be a sequel and there will always be a reboot, because names are the safest way to make your financial return. It is a huge risk to invest a whole lot of money in an original IP, so nonoriginal IPs are always your safest bet for making money. If you're looking at commercially driven narrative products or creative products there's always going to be a sequel...unless it's *Bulletstorm*, unfortunately. The most interesting narrative stuff in games is happening beyond Triple-A and has been for a very long time, and that's because there are less people on the team and the same primary motivators do not drive them—namely, advanced technological spectacle, systemic complexity, and 80 hours of "gameplay." They're driven by, "I want to tell thing, so I'm going to tell this thing." When I teach game development to students, they all come in having only played Triple-A games and the most commercial indie titles, and it's really hard because none of those games are useful for them as starting out game developers, or as people who are interested in game narrative. That is not where interesting game narrative is happening, unfortunately, and it's not where interesting game narrative *can* happen. The real issue in video games is that Triple-A is seen as the default most prestigious place games happen. Even when I talk about indie or Triple-A, people are then thinking about *Fez* or *Super Meat Boy* or *Minecraft*, which is just the tip of the iceberg. If you look at a site like itch.io, which is like Steam for everything else, there's so much more experimental stuff out there and so much more valuable stuff out there. For people who want to express themselves through their video games and want to tell their own story, they're much better off going at looking at a game engine like Twine, or Bitsy, and making their own little 5-min story with that. The challenge is that people, when all they've played is Triple-A, think these 5-min-long games with lo-fi and zero systemic complexity are bad, simply because they're not what Triple-A says is good. What Triple-A says is good are the games that only Triple-A has the ability and resources to make. This has been the strategy of the industry since the 1980s, ever since Nintendo took over the US after the game development crash of Atari. The opinion was that the industry crashed because there was too much amateur stuff out there, so they decided to make it harder for amateurs to get their stuff out there. They did that on the NES with the 10NES chip and Quality of Assurance seal of approval, as well as really strict editorial guidelines of what it would take to get on a console. This meant that from the mid-1980s to the mid-2000s, indie games were essentially invisible. The industry wanted them to be invisible, and it wasn't until broadband Internet allowed indie games to circumvent the industry that we started seeing these games again. By that point, it was very much normalized what a good video game was, and this is why when we try to talk about good narrative in games, we just default to talking about good narrative in Triple-A games, as if that's the space it needs to be validated or seen. Really, video games solved the narrative problem a long time ago; it's just not happening in the commercial space. What I tell my students is: you don't need to go and play *Breath of the Wild* for 80 hours. That won't teach you anything about video game narrative that you won't learn in the first 5 min of that game. Instead, go and play 100 5-min games on itch.io, all of which are free, and you'll learn so much more about narrative and design in video games.

5

This is Snake
The Storytelling Legacy of the Metal Gear *Series*

For casual and hardcore gamers alike Konami Digital Entertainment's *Metal Gear* series, helmed by series director Hideo Kojima and consisting of 21 titles since 1987, is infamous for jarring breaks in the fourth wall, extended cutscenes and convoluted, often even contradictory, narrative threads. These hallmarks of the franchise have rendered it a beloved classic for many and a niche curiosity for many more. In this chapter, I will explore moments in the *Metal Gear* series where narrative and play intersect. Framed using analysis from my personal play-through of the series, these are moments that disrupt preconceived notions of ludonarrative dissonance.[1] The act of playing as *Metal Gear*'s central player-characters, the heroes collectively known as Snake, engages with three tenets of video game play: limitation, identity, and iteration. *Metal Gear*'s creative interrogation of these three tenets suggests a blueprint for games writing where narrative and play can operate in symbiosis.

As prefaced in this book's introduction, using the personal play-through as an analytical tool accesses the unique experience of the singular player. This chapter therefore begins with my earliest memories of the *Metal Gear* series and an introductory analysis that highlights one example of how narrative and play intersect in a video game. These tenets of video game play, limitation, identity, and iteration are then taken to task in each subsequent analysis as tools able to bridge the potential gap between narrative and play.

---

[1] See this book's introduction for a brief explanation of Clint Hocking's "ludonarrative dissonance."

Metal Gear Solid's (*MGS1*) Psycho Mantis boss encounter reflexively plays with the limitations of video games imposed by the physical setup of the video game system as well as the inherent distance between the player and the player-character. In furthering my analysis of the series, I look at *Metal Gear Solid 2: Sons of Liberty* (*MGS2*) where playing as Raiden confounds the identity of the player and their control of the player-character. This chapter then closes with an analysis of the final tenet, iteration. The existence of save-states and game-overs means that each play-through of any game is unavoidably iterative, but for *Metal Gear*, each entry into the series also iterates on previous entries, establishing repetition as yet another tenet of play able to be creatively explored.

As children, my older brother and I subscribed to the *Official PlayStation 2 Magazine*, and what we coveted above all else was the front cover demo disc. In 2004, during one such demo disc misadventure, I encountered the *Metal Gear* series in the soon-to-be-released *Metal Gear Solid 3: Snake Eater* (*MGS3*). *MGS3* is the third game in the *Solid* series; however, it is set in 1964 making it the first title within the chronological fiction of the *Metal Gear* universe. Naked Snake is *MGS3*'s player-character, and thus, the first Snake I ever played as was, coincidentally, the first to take up the moniker. I say "first Snake" because every installment in the series has players control a character codenamed Snake. Needless to say things are going to get confusing, try to keep up.

According to the magazine's feature article, *MGS3* could be classified as a stealth-shooter game with dynamic jungle survival elements. The series by-line is "Tactical Espionage Action," and, as Naked Snake, players take on the role of a special operations soldier assigned with sneaking into enemy compounds, stealing secrets, and evading capture. The game boasted varying weather effects, contextual camouflage, injury and stamina meters, advanced enemy AI, and an impressive roster of jungle wildlife to trap and hunt.

My brother and I sat upon the white shag carpet of our lounge room in suburban Melbourne and booted up the *MGS3* demo. It begins with Snake sitting in the back of a US Military cargo plane readying himself for a HALO (high altitude, low open) parachute jump. Of course, he can't start the mission until he begrudgingly stubs out his cigar. It is the kind of narrative opening that would make John Carpenter blush. Indeed, Snake's namesake and esthetic are borrowed from Snake Plissken, the cynical and reluctant hero from Carpenter's *Escape from New York* (1981) and *Escape from L.A.* (1996). After receiving orders from Major Zero, Snake inches out over the open cargo ramp and makes the jump. He plummets through the air, pulls his chute, and lands on a rocky outcrop in the jungles of Tselinoyarsk in the USSR. The tactical insertion opening would have been familiar to fans of the series; it's an opening that has announced every *Metal Gear* to date, almost always followed by a familiar line, "This is Snake."

Snake takes cover in some shrubs and kneels down to patch in his field radio, known across the series as the codec—this is an item players can use at any time to converse with the various characters that form Snake's support team. The screen fades to black and then fades again into the codec view; Snake is kneeling on the right-hand side of the screen, while Major Zero's small portrait and radio frequency appear on the left. What follows is a further 3 min of mission briefing and intel relay, this on top of the 8-min opening cutscene. With little patience, my brother skips most of this, and finally, we are playing once more. Our objective is to retrieve Snake's backpack that was snagged on a tree during the parachute landing. This proves simple enough, and we complete this objective in only half a minute, prompting another call on the codec. This time we listen to an additional 9 min of complex briefing, intel, and back story.

The Boss: Jack, is that you? How many years has it been?
   Snake: Boss?
The Boss: That's right, it's me.
   Snake: …
The Boss: Talk to me, let me hear your voice.
   Snake: It's been 5 years, 72 days, and 18 hours.
The Boss: You've lost weight.
   Snake: You can tell just by the sound of my voice?
The Boss: Of course I can. I know all about you.
   Snake: Really? Well, I don't know anything about you.
The Boss: What's that supposed to mean?
   Snake: Why'd you disappear on me all of a sudden?
The Boss: I was on a top-secret mission.
   Snake: …
The Boss: You didn't need me anymore.
   Snake: But there were still so many things I wanted you to teach me.
The Boss: No. I taught you everything you needed to know about fighting techniques. I taught you all I could. The rest you needed to learn on your own.
   Snake: Techniques sure, but what about how to think like a soldier?

The Boss: How to think like a soldier? I can't teach you that. A soldier needs to be strong in spirit, body, and technique, and the only thing you can learn from someone else is technique. In fact, technique doesn't even matter. What's most important is spirit. Spirit and body are like two sides of a single coin; they're the same thing. I can't teach you how to think. You'll just have to figure it out for yourself. Listen to me, Jack, just because soldiers are on the same side right now doesn't mean they always will be. Having personal feelings about your comrades is one the worst sins you can commit. Politics determine who you face on the battlefield, and politics are a living thing: they change along with the times. Yesterday's good might be tomorrow's evil.

Snake: Is that why you abandoned me?

(©Konami Digital Entertainment. With permission)

We are eager to progress past these cutscenes, and eventually we do. Snake is tasked with navigating the jungle paths to a Russian research facility. We set out to do just this when we hit a roadblock: enemy soldiers on the path ahead. The next half hour is punctuated with sighs, yells, and an abandonment of the controller in disgust. I take over and I too am unable to sneak past the game's very first enemies and promptly give up. We jointly decide that it's the fault of the fixed camera angles, the poor equip item function, the wonky detection system—it's the game's fault, certainly not the players.

I find it appropriate that both the narrative and gameplay challenges that stopped me from embracing the series when I was younger are the same challenges that many have come up against in their experiences across the series. The cutscenes and codec conversations are evidently ambitious, and the back-stories for each game's characters are fastidious in their attention to detail. Even now I find the boldly camp content and delivery of the series often impenetrable; Rob Gallagher notes that *Metal Gear*'s attempts to "baulk, baffle, or obstruct" are part of an inherent eroticism associated with all video game play but especially suited to a series that "encourag[es] players to cultivate a pleasure in dalliance and indirection" (2012). Eroticism aside, this tone of baffling difficulty stretches across the series to the point that failure, a fact of play strongly associated with the iterative nature of games, becomes thematised (Juul, 2013; Youngblood, 2017).[2] Similarly, the series

---

[2] A specific and now oft-cited example of such is *MGS2*'s "Fission Mailed" game-over screen. For further discussion on the narrative potentials of failure, see our Chapter 6 interview with Anna Anthropy.

refuses to make concessions in the difficulty of mastering its gameplay. My original 2004 experience of story and gameplay in *MGS3* was one of barriers. For my 12-year-old self, these difficulty barriers were a detriment that pushed the game into obscurity. More than a decade later and now, I believe that these moments of intersection between narrative and play are consistent storytelling tools spanning the breadth of the *Metal Gear* series.

I've chosen in this chapter to discuss the numbered canonical installments from the *Solid* series: this includes *Metal Gear Solid, Metal Gear Solid 2: Sons of Liberty, Metal Gear Solid 3: Snake Eater, Metal Gear Solid 4: Guns of the Patriots*, and *Metal Gear Solid V: Ground Zeroes/The Phantom Pain*. I have not included the canonical original *Metal Gear 1* and *2* (from which the series was launched) and the PSP title *Metal Gear Solid: Peace Walker*. This barely touches on Konami's noncanonical entries, spin-offs, legacy editions, pachinko remasters, and portable titles. Confused yet? Perhaps a table could help (Figure 5.1):

FIGURE 5.1
The *Metal Gear Solid* series

Release Year	Title	Fictional Chronology
1987	**Metal Gear**	1995
1990	Snake's Revenge	1998
1990	**Metal Gear 2: Solid Snake**	1999
1998	**Metal Gear Solid**	2005
2000	Metal Gear: Ghost Babel	1994
2001	**Metal Gear Solid 2: Sons of Liberty**	2007/09
2004	Metal Gear Solid: The Twin Snakes (An *MGS1* remaster)	2005
2004	**Metal Gear Solid 3: Snake Eater**	1964
2004	Metal Gear Acid	2016
2005	Metal Gear Acid 2	2016
2006	**Metal Gear Solid: Portable ops**	1970
2007	Metal Gear Solid: Portable Ops Plus	1970
2008	Metal Gear Solid Touch	2014
2008	Metal Gear Solid Mobile	2006
2008	**Metal Gear Solid 4: Guns of the Patriots**	2014
2010	**Metal Gear Solid: Peace Walker**	1974
2013	**Metal Gear Rising: Revengeance**	2018
2014	**Metal Gear Solid V: Ground Zeroes**	1975
2015	**Metal Gear Solid V: The Phantom Pain**	1984
2016	Metal Gear Solid Snake Eater, Pachislot	1964
2018	Metal Gear Survive	1975

Titles in Bold are Considered Canonical to the Main Series as Designated by Series Director/Writer Hideo Kojima.

Or perhaps not—fortunately, what this table does make clear is the density and volume of the *Metal Gear* series. An attempt to discuss all of it would far exceed the scope of this chapter. Indeed, even my attempt to discuss a fraction of the series means leaving large swathes of information out. The behind-the-scenes development of the series has also been storied and nuanced. Kojima, a man who is a rock star of the games industry, has helmed the *Metal Gear* series since its inception. As exclusive developers of the *Metal Gear* series, Kojima Productions was founded in 2005 under its parent company Konami Digital Entertainment. Kojima Productions, however, was then disbanded and reformed as an independent studio in 2015 citing creative differences. Crucially though, Kojima Productions parted with the *Metal Gear* series during this turmoil handing full creative control over to Konami. In light of all this, it is true that many hardcore fans consider a *Metal Gear* game without Kojima at the helm hardly a *Metal Gear* game at all, so critical is his directorial vision. A hardcore fan myself I'm inclined to agree, while I'm tentative to commit to the term auteur I'm not afraid to suggest that the powerful legacy of storytelling tools present in the series owes a tremendous debt to Kojima's vision.[3] Even if Kojima himself remains sheepish about how this vision transfers to his audience, he plainly considers video game storytelling a complex balancing act between gameplay and narrative:

> I believe that even today we can only tell a simple story without really interfering with gameplay. But in the future I think it will almost be a requirement of all storytellers when they create games, how they can tell a more complex story without conflicting with the gameplay.
>
> (Rose, 2009)

In *Metal Gear Solid* (*MGS1*), this balancing act becomes most apparent during the Psycho Mantis boss fight—an encounter that exposes the limitations of the video game play. In this title, players assume the role of Solid Snake, one of three soldiers cloned from the genes of Naked Snake. As far as typical boss fights go, the encounter is fiendishly difficult: Solid Snake is trapped in a small square office with only two side tables and a desk to take cover behind. Psycho Mantis, a telepath able to read minds, hovers from one side of the room to the other telekinetically launching objects at the player. Mantis begins the fight by reading the player's memory card; in my play-through, there was unfortunately not much for him but if players have saved files from other

---

[3] Consult our interviews with Anna Anthropy in Chapter 6 and Brendan Keogh in Chapter 4 for discussions on the role of the auteur in game studies.

Konami titles such as *Azure Dreams* (1997) or *Castlevania: Symphony of the Night* (1997), among others, he will comment on their good taste. Similarly, Mantis commended my "prudent" nature as I'd saved the game three or more times before reaching the encounter. If players have saved less than three times, Mantis will scold them for being "reckless." Mantis also makes use of a now often referenced trick where he reads the player's controller and is able to dodge incoming attacks with agile indifference (Conway, 2010; Keogh, 2014; Dunne, 2014). One of only two ways to counter this move, a counter that took me far too long to figure out, is to unplug the controller from Port 1 and reassign it to Port 2. Additionally, as a demonstration of his colossal power, Mantis tells players "put your controller on the floor… now I will move your controller by the power of my will alone," using the controllers vibrations he moves it from left to right. Mantis' moves here demonstrate a parallel between Snake's story and the player's story, and in doing so, they highlight the inter-section between narrative and play.[4]

Psycho Mantis' big ruse though is his ability to interrupt the fight by changing the screen to a fake video input screen; this is a black screen with green text in the top right corner that reads "HIDEO," as opposed to "VIDEO." Upon seeing this screen for the first time, players are meant to assume the console has crashed and that they are seeing the television's awaiting video input screen. During my first encounter with Mantis, I was blind-sided by this fake glitch and promptly pressed the reset button on my console—only when it happened again at the same moment did I realize my error. These ludic tweaks of gameplay and explicit nods to hardware have narrative payoff. Mantis is more dangerous and terrifying as a character because of his ability to close the distance between the player's avatar, Snake, and the player themselves. The players' journey with Snake has "no past [and] no future;" Mantis' implication is that players' only frame of reference for knowing Snake is through the present and thus through play. In narrowing this distance, the limitations of video games as a medium are made apparent: namely, these tricks remind players that this is *just* a game and that try as they might to be Snake players can only ever play at becoming Snake.

Psycho Mantis: I can read people's minds. In my lifetime, I have read the pasts, presents, and futures of thousands upon thousands of men and women… and each mind that I peered into was

---

[4]In Chapter 4, Brendan Keogh discusses these limitations in a similar manner. He also highlights the gimmicky, and yet somehow not game-breaking, nature of the fight.

stuffed with the same single object of obsession. That selfish and atavistic desire to pass on one's seed… it was enough to make me sick. Every living thing on this planet exists to mindlessly pass on their DNA. We're designed that way, and that's why there is war. But you, you are different; you're the same as us. We have no past, no future. We live in the moment, that's our only purpose. Humans weren't designed to bring each other happiness. From the moment we're thrown into this world, we're fated to bring each other nothing but pain and misery. The first person whose mind I dove into was my father's. I saw nothing but disgust and hatred for me in his heart. My mother died in childbirth and he despised me for it, I thought my father was going to kill me. That's when my future disappeared. I lost my past as well. When I came to, the village was engulfed in flames.

Snake: Are you saying you burned your village down to bury your past?

Psycho Mantis: I see that you have suffered the same trauma. We are truly the same, you and I. The world is a more interesting place with people like you in it. I've seen true evil. You Snake, you're just like the Boss… no, you're worse. Compared to you, I'm not so bad.

(©Konami Digital Entertainment. With permission)

Mantis expertly disrupts the fourth wall, creating both identification and alienation simultaneously. Steven Conway discusses this device of video game characters breaking the fourth wall. Conway states that the existence of the player is problematic for the traditional idea of the fourth wall as the player fulfills "the dual role of audience member and performer" (2010). This continual feedback loop renders any kind of conceptual wall obsolete. In other words, the act of playing has already broken and continues to perpetually break the fourth wall. Therefore, Conway proposes the metaphor of a circle instead of a wall that either expands or contracts to, respectively, amplify or disrupt this feedback loop. Conway calls this the "magic circle:" a term that instantly conveys the sense of fantasy achieved when a player is immersed within the circle, and when they are thrust outside of it.

Conway identifies an example of the circle expanding in *MGS1* when Naomi Hunter, Snake's medical advisor, contacts him via codec and suggests he place the controller upon the nape of his neck as he seems stressed.

Seconds later the controller vibrates, simulating a massage supposed to calm Snake down. Naomi's mention and subsequent manipulation of the player's controller explicitly repositions the player as a figure within the narrative. Players are still Snake, but they are also a player sitting on a couch goofily holding a vibrating controller to their neck. As Conway writes:

> [This example illustrates] not the breaking of the fourth wall in the traditional sense, as it is not actively shattering the suspension of disbelief, but instead how the fourth wall is itself relocated, enhancing the sense of immersion, as it is moved from in front of the player to behind him or her, and he or she is drawn further into the fictional universe of the gameworld, which now encompasses the technology of the television set or game control pad.
>
> *(2010)*

The game's acknowledgment of the player does not necessarily break our personal investment in the game but enhances it. When I first encountered this scene, I didn't actually do as Naomi Hunter suggested. I instead sat on the couch completely dumbfounded because I just couldn't fathom that she was addressing me and not Snake, or rather, that she was addressing both of us. As the game slowly revealed itself to me though, I began to relish these small moments where the circle was repositioned and my distance from Snake reduced. These moments with Psycho Mantis and Naomi Hunter, among others, heralded my involvement within the story: they were instances where the "fiction [became] momentarily tangible" (Conway, 2010). In this sense, exposing the limitations of the medium is one method the *Metal Gear* series uses to enhance player involvement and merge the potentially disparate worlds of narrative and play.

In *Metal Gear Solid 2: Sons of Liberty*, identity and identification, from player to player-character, becomes muddled in a deliberate attempt to again force narrative and play into a partnership. *MGS2* was a hotly debated entry to the franchise upon release, as many fans felt deceived by a marketing bait-and-switch regarding the central player-character (Youngblood, 2017). In the first chapter of the game, this also being the prerelease demo level and the source of the vast majority of marketing material, players presumed they would control series mainstay Solid Snake (the hero of *Metal Gear 1* and *2* as well as *MGS1* and, later, *MGS4*). However, the remaining 90% of the game sees players control not Solid Snake but a new character: the lithe, androgynous Raiden. Raiden's first appearance and reveal to players is slow and is close to a shot-for-shot recreation of Solid Snake's introduction in *MGS1*.

Toward the end of the game, it is revealed to Raiden that his entire mission has been a carefully orchestrated plot designed to mimic the events of *MGS1* and create a soldier equal to the skill of Solid Snake. In *MGS2*, Raiden and, in turn, I fight for agency against this orchestration. Both fights with Solidus Snake, the third clone produced from Naked Snake and the principal antagonist of the game, showcase this agency in its two forms—ludic and narrative.

Agency is a powerful tool that, due to the fact it hinges on the player, is often core to discussions of game design. Player agency commonly emerges as the ideal state of play that game designers strive to elicit. Espen Aarseth touches on player agency in his formulation of video games as an ergodic medium, a medium that must be actively traversed along its "workable path" (1997). I'd like to add to this Jesper Juul's establishment of what a game is at its basic coding level: "a rule-based system with a variable and quantifiable outcome" ([2005] 2011). Some outcomes are quantifiably bad, the player-character is injured or dies, and some are good, the player-character is rewarded emotionally, physically, or otherwise. Juul and Aarseth together dictate the game as a set of rules manipulated by the player's "nontrivial effort" (Aarseth, 1997). I have been careful to lay the groundwork of these definitions not so that I can categorize games versus not-games, but so that it is clear that the player agency exerted upon a game world is a dual act of immersion and active control. If players can maintain this immersion and active control while achieving quantifiably good outcomes, then they can, theoretically, experience agency.[5] In a less theoretical summary: agency is the feeling that this is my story, that I am in control, and that every action is happening not because the game wills it but because I do.

Evidencing ludic agency, or agency through gameplay, is the first Solidus Snake boss encounter of *MGS2* during which Solidus pilots a Harrier jet. During the encounter, the Harrier jet behaves predictably, its flight path is not random and its attacks are easy to anticipate—the game only asks that the player learn the move-set of the enemy. Solidus' various yells throughout the fight signal different things to the player, "You're tougher than I thought" is an indication that Solidus is preparing to unleash a barrage of rockets. If the player has learnt this about Solidus, then taking cover from this fire is relatively simple and the player can take no damage. This formulaic behavior is a way of teaching the player; while the player may die the

---

[5] Janet Murray's evaluation of agency as a Deleuzian rhizome is equally as helpful here. It is, however, a narrative-centric approach that struggles to holistically consider video games as multi-disciplinary (1997).

first or even second time Solidus telegraphs his intention to strike, chances are they will pick up on these verbal cues and behave accordingly. Thus, the game is imparting agency to the player and forcing the player to learn from his or her own mistakes. This sense of reward at the cost of learning is the key to boss encounters; it suggests that progression through the game world is only achievable if the player learns how to manipulate it.

This manipulation can extend to a transgression of the game rules. In one particularly obvious swoop attack, Solidus will bombard the gangway with multiple missiles at the same time. A player familiar with the mechanics of the game can avoid this attack entirely, as opposed to taking a large amount of damage, by pressing the jump button at the gangway rail. Doing so will launch the player-character over the side of the gangway in a prescribed animation, and Raiden will hang on to the opposite side of the railing. This prescribed animation takes roughly ten frames, or a quarter of a second, and during it, the player is immune to damage. This immunity affords the player invincibility frames, and while it is most likely a coding oversight (read: glitch), it is a move that can be abused in order to defeat the Harrier jet much quicker than would otherwise be possible. It should be noted that this is not a technique I myself discovered, and while I have played around with it a little, it proves extraordinarily difficult to pull off. The combination of correct timing as well as familiarity with the game itself reserves this technique for the professionals.

Harvey Smith, lead designer for the critically successful *Deus Ex* (2000), outlines his design team's intentions in "allow[ing] the player to come up with his own strategies within the flexible rules of the environment" (p. 2). This is a strategy that Smith claims led to emergent gameplay, a concept that produced desirable and undesirable gameplay solutions. Smith contends that the moments when players transgress these rules are failures of design and are "more about what the designer want[s] the player to do" as opposed to "what the player want[s] to do" (p. 3). Smith's discussion of these player transgressions is a demonstrable link to player agency; the invincibility frames trick of the Harrier boss encounter is an example of a player using one set of rules to break another, they are pitting the game world against itself. Players able to achieve quantifiably good outcomes while still maintaining immersion and active control have effectively secured independent agency within the game world.

The above example of the Harrier fight is ludic agency. There is some narrative payoff in that the player feels they truly are the capable hero the game wants them to be, but for the most part the player is manipulating the game for the game's sake. Perhaps the more important question to ask is how

FIGURE 5.2
Questioning the limits of player agency in *MGS2*

The Purposely Glitched Codec with a Skull Overlaid on the Colonel's Face on the Left. (©Konami Digital Entertainment. With permission).

a player can achieve agency in a narrative sense. The final boss fight of the game, again versus Solidus Snake, is an answer to this question.

This fight is a complicated and difficult, analyzing it means considering all that comes before it. I'll do my best to spare you the messy, and frankly confusing, details. What follows is my play-through of this boss fight, and evidently just one interpretation.

Raiden has just escaped interrogation and torture at the hands of Solidus Snake. He is completely naked and running through the underbelly of Arsenal Gear, an enormous robot on a collision course with New York City. The Colonel, whom Raiden has been receiving orders from via codec the entire game, has started spouting nonsense, and the codec itself is showing signs of glitches (Figure 5.2).

I let out a genuine sigh of relief when Solid Snake appears behind Raiden. He has been helping Raiden throughout the game, both in the field and on the codec, and this time is no different. Snake gives Raiden some clothes and also gives him a new weapon—the high frequency (HF) blade. The HF blade is a weapon, something like a tech-modded samurai sword, which Solid Snake himself has never wielded. Snake has something more to add though, he reveals that cerebral implants have given Raiden a false memory; in addition to this, the Colonel is actually an AI construct controlled by a shadowy cabal known as The Patriots. This Illuminati-esque group has carefully railroaded the entire plot of the game, and their goal is to have Raiden kill Solidus Snake in an effort to create the perfect supersoldier—"a hero to surpass Solid Snake." Everything has been lies, deceit and trickery, not just perpetrated against Raiden but against me too. Of course, I still feel a compulsion to confront Solidus Snake, he claims to have known Raiden in a former life before his false memories, and he also claims to be an estranged mentor and father figure. Even if Raiden weren't naked, the metaphor is self-evident: this is Raiden's birthing scene as a new hero. He is shrugging off the lies and taking up a new weapon and a new resolve. He'll need both if he is to defeat Solidus Snake and uncover the truth about his origins.

The glitching Colonel tells Raiden about how he saw a UFO last Thursday as he was driving home and his codec picture switches between faces before being overlaid with a skull. I shrug him off and continue forward. Snake and I make for the roof of Arsenal Gear, deftly removing the enemies in our path. There are some misdirections and extended cutscenes, a man named Revolver Ocelot lays out the Patriots' plan in painstaking detail before he hijacks a nuclear-armed robot, this being one of the many titular "Metal Gear" mechs, which the series is known for, and flees. Snake takes off after him just as Arsenal Gear reaches its destination and crashes headlong into Federal Hall, New York. Once the dust settles, I find it's just Raiden and Solidus alone atop the roof of Federal Hall. This is it, the final showdown.

This fight is the most difficult I've yet faced, it involves precision timing, and when Solidus hits, he hits hard. Over the next few minutes, we duke it out; I whittle away at his health bar reducing it sliver by sliver until finally I'm sure that there are just one or two more strikes until he is down for good. Solidus charges, I dodge and then quickly close the distance on his unsuspecting right side—cue cutscene.

The fight is suddenly narrative in nature. As Will has pointed out in his analysis of *The Last of Us* (2013), in games, linear narrative's chief tool is the cutscene. Framed according to cinematic conventions, cutscenes take complete control away from the player and depict the player-character talking and moving independently. During these sequences, the player-character can become wounded or even killed. Most importantly, these cutscenes are often irreversible; the cutscene is a permanent story progression that deliberately excludes the player, and with that permanence comes narrative power. Rune Klevjer understands cutscenes as "a conflict of agency […] a balancing and a struggle between the agency of the story-game and the agency of the player" (Klevjer, 2002, p. 10). More accurately phrased, Klevjer's conclusions on cutscenes could be considered a struggle between narrative and play. The cutscene is the game at its most narrative heavy, and its least ergodic. In this nonplayable sequence, Raiden deftly sidesteps a charge from Solidus, just as I had done moments before, and swings his sword in a bloody arc down the

center of Solidus Snake's spine. Matthew Weise describes this cutscene inter-
ruption as a deliberate "violation of [player] agency" (Weise, 2003, p. 13).

While it is accurate to suggest that the player's ludic agency has been vio-
lated, I'll suggest that a second type of agency, narrative agency, persists. Weise
totalizes cutscenes as completely devoid of player agency stating that Raiden,
and by extension the player, "has no agency other than what his puppet masters give him" (Weise, 2003, p. 13). In his breakdown of the 2005 release *Peter
Jackson's King Kong: The Official Game of the Movie*, Paul Cheng discusses
how "limit[ing] player interactivity […] actually increases a sense of player
agency" (Cheng, 2007, p. 21). Cheng is dissecting a different kind of cutscene,
a first person cutscene where players never leave the point of view of the player-
character. The differences between this cutscene and the penultimate moment
of *MGS2* are numerous; however, Cheng observes one unifying point:

> [L]imitations imposed upon the player are not due to any arbitrary
> reason of game mechanics, but [arise] from a situation that makes
> logical sense in the gameworld.
>
> *(p. 21)*

The violation of ludic agency at the point where Raiden delivers the killing
blow is a logical progression of this game world. Raiden's lot is to be manipulated: he is manipulated by the Patriots, manipulated by Solidus Snake,
manipulated by Solid Snake, manipulated by almost every one of his codec
contacts, and of course he is manipulated by me—the player. That control of
Raiden should be snatched away from me at this pivotal point is only fitting.
Raiden's character arc and birth as a hero is dependent on his independence.
This is only further proven when Raiden walks away from the battle in the
final scene and pulls a set of dog tags from around his neck. Solid Snake asks,
"Anyone you know?" to which Raiden responds, "No, never heard the name
before." Of course, the name imprinted on the tags is my name, the name of
the player. I'd entirely forgotten I entered these details at the very start of the
game and am taken aback. Raiden throws the tags into the street, "I'll pick
my own name, and my own life. I'll find something worth passing on." This
moment implicates the player within the game world and delivers both narrative consistency as well as ergodic activity. Admittedly, it is just a whisper, but
there is narrative agency here underneath this cutscene. The consistency of
the narrative logically strips me of my ability to play and forces me to engage
in a kind of not-play. Paul Cheng positions narrative agency; similarly, "the
question of 'meaningful action' can easily be described as 'meaningful inac-
tion (2007).'" True to the espionage genre *MGS2* enacts a violence of belief

and exposes player/player-character identification as fundamentally impossible. In the same way that Pyscho Mantis uses the act of play itself to uncover the medium's inherent limitations, *MGS2* suggests that in order for Raiden, or any player-character, to fulfill their heroic narrative arc they must graduate beyond the players control and become more than a "[pawn] in a game."

> *Solidus:* Liquid and Solid hunted down Big Boss, trying to sever the tie that bound them to him. Unless you kill me and face your past, Jack, you will never escape. You'll stay in the endless loop – your own double helix. It's time we were both free.
> [Raiden gets a Codec call from the Colonel.]
> *Colonel:* Raiden, you have to beat Solidus! This is your last duty!
> *Raiden:* We're not just pawns in some simulation game, you know!
> *Rose:* Yes, you are. You're nothing but mere weapons. No different from fighter jets or tanks.
> *Raiden:* What the...
> *Colonel:* The old model destroyed 4 years ago was "REX"...
> *Rose:* The new amphibious model is "RAY"...
> *Colonel:* Both of these are the same as the code names used by the U.S. Armed Forces to refer to Japanese war-planes during World War II.
> *Rose:* Your code name "Raiden" too comes from the Japanese navy's name for one of its interceptors.
> *Raiden:* Stop it! I'm not a weapon!
> *Colonel:* Oh really? Do you know the code name the U.S. Armed Forces used for the Japanese fighter "Raiden?"
> *Rose:* It was "Jack."
> *Colonel:* Both of you are just weapons to be used and thrown away.
> *Rose:* Just weapons to be used on the battlefield. Just pawns in a game – exactly as you said.
> *Colonel:* And a weapon has no right to think for itself! Now, it's time to fulfill your purpose! Defeat Solidus!
> *(©Konami Digital Entertainment. With permission)*

By the time *Metal Gear Solid 4: Guns of the Patriots* (*MGS4*) released in 2008, the series was already well established as a bastion of the stealth genre and had come to define what many called the postmodern video game (Rogers, 2007; Myles, 2012; Stanton, 2015). The loaded implications of this term are numerous, yet it's clear that the series' ability to reflexively engage with the limitations of its form as well as tackle themes like player/player-character identification had positioned it as a meta-game, a game about games. *Metal Gear Solid 4: Guns of the Patriots* (*MGS4*) and *Metal Gear Solid V: Ground Zeroes/The Phantom Pain* (*MGSV: GZ/ MGSV: TPP*) are evidence of storytelling tools that have evolved beyond exposing limitations of the form or upsetting notions of identity. Instead, these titles tackle the iterative nature of video games, positioning repetition at the intersection of narrative and play. I will close this chapter with an analysis of how these final titles in the series continued to iterate on past titles, a cyclical refinement of a formula designed to establish a legacy of new storytelling within video games.

Where previously Psycho Mantis simply alluded to the fact that a controller existed, in *MGS4*, Solid Snake actually carries a Dualshock 3 as a part of his gear. The Dualshock 3, which is Sony's fancy name for the controller paired with the Playstation 3 system, is used by Snake to manipulate a small sentry bot. This bot, the Metal Gear Mk.II, can give Snake eyes in places he otherwise wouldn't be able to reach. So as I manipulate Snake with my Dualshock 3, he manipulates the Mk.II with his Dualshock 3. Conway again recognizes this as the "obsession with console hardware rear[ing] its head" (Conway, 2010, p. 149). Here, our real world objects are leaking into the game and blurring the boundaries.

This is doubly so for both installments of *MGSV* where the leak appears to travel both ways, with various pieces of gear and apparel appearing in the game that have real-life counterparts. Snake's iDROID (an anachronistic portmanteau of iPhone and Android) is a small personal computer used to review intel and contact home base. Following the games publication, Japanese fans were able to buy iDROID phone cases complete with light-up LEDs. Paired with *MGSV*'s second-screen phone application, an app that allows players to view the map, request ammunition, and call for evac, players might also be holding an actual iDROID. In a similar vein, the game's release concurrently saw the release of an exclusive line of J.F Rey sunglasses and optical frames specially designed to filter the harsh blue light emitted by television screens. Whenever these glasses appear in game on the faces of various hero characters, the camera takes a special moment to zoom in and focus on the frames as the model and manufacturer flash across the screen. These moments strike me as far more than a simple repositioning of the magic circle; the obsession here is not just with the console hardware but also with all video game merchandise. The player is no longer just implied but is instead narratively embedded within the framework of how this story is being told.

As mentioned earlier, prior to *MGS2*'s release fans were led to believe they would be returning to the battlefield as Solid Snake instead of the dramatically different Raiden. This bait-and-switch would return in both *MGS4* and *MGSV*. Solid Snake last appeared as an operative in his prime in *MGS2*, 5 years later during the events of *MGS4* and Solid Snake have become Old Snake, his natural lifespan as a clone of Naked Snake/Big Boss has afflicted him with accelerated ageing and he now possesses the body of a man in his mid-60s. While players were aware of Solid Snake's return as Old Snake, what was not immediately obvious was just how damaged Snake's failing clone body had become. Snake's body has white hair paired with a bushy white moustache, and he is constantly complaining of aches and pains. Leaving Old Snake idle will have him rub and bemoan the various sore spots on his back. In this way, playing Snake in *MGS4* comes with the tragic implication that we are also slowly killing him. This is displayed quite literally when Old Snake must crawl through a lethal microwave corridor in order to confront the final boss.

In a similar fashion, *MGSV: TPP* attempts a far bolder bait-and-switch through convincing players they really are playing as Big Boss, formerly Naked Snake, until Mission 46 of 50. This mission is called "Truth—The Man Who Sold the World," and in it, players are required to replay the prologue with a series of subtle differences. The cutscene that closes this mission reveals that the real Big Boss has been in hiding during the events of the game and that players have actually been in charge of Venom Snake, a surgically altered body double under the spell of hypnotherapy. This echoes the closing moments of *MGS2*—at first Raiden believed he was Snake, then he was trying to become Snake, and finally, he was a soldier willing to become something he himself would choose. This choice for the body double at the end of *MGSV: TPP*, codenamed Venom Snake, is to continue to live the lie and become a phantom of Big Boss. In both instances, the player's agency is compromised, and the question of who is controlling what hangs in the air. Just as Raiden and Venom Snake cannot in fact become Solid Snake or Big Boss, respectively, players are also forced to remain as the player figure. In this sense, the player's journey in every iteration of the series mirrors the journey of Raiden and Venom Snake. Players and player-characters alike play to become Snake, yet this is shown to be a goal that consistently eludes the grasp of both.

> *Big Boss:* Now do you remember? Who are you? What you were meant to do? I cheated death thanks to you, and thanks to you I've left my mark. You have too, you've written your own history, you're your own man. I'm Big Boss, and you are too... no, he's the two of us together. Where we are today, we built it. This story, this legend, it's ours. We can change the world and with it the future. I am you and you are me, carry that with you wherever you go. Thank you, my friend. From here on out, you're Big Boss.
>
> *(©Konami Digital Entertainment. With permission)*

Similarly, the boss fights in these later installments echo the boss challenges of games past. In *MGS4*, all seven main bosses have either been fought in a previous game or their names and abilities pay homage to past boss characters. There are four members of The Beauty and The Beast Corps, codenamed: Laughing Octopus, Raging Raven, Crying Wolf, and Screaming Mantis. These bosses represent the six emotions personified by the Cobra Unit bosses of *MGS3*: The Joy, The Fury, The Sorrow, The End, The Pain, and The Fear. Similarly, the nouns in their codenames are references to *MGS1* bosses Decoy Octopus, Vulcan Raven, Sniper Wolf, and Psycho Mantis. And finally, their abilities match the skills of *MGS2*'s Solidus Snake, Fatman, Fortune, and Vamp. While this could easily be considered creative bankruptcy, for me the repetition instead plays out like a museum exhibition of consideration and appreciation.[6]

MGS4's final encounter with Liquid Ocelot is something of a mash-up between fighting Revolver Ocelot and the psyche that has apparently possessed him, *MGS1*'s Liquid Snake. As players whittle down each section of Liquid Ocelot's life bar, the name below that life bar will change to reflect the persona Snake is currently dueling with. First players fight the "Liquid" persona whose fighting style and mocking quips match Liquid Snake, as this phase ends the real Liquid's face flashes across the screen and is then replaced by that of Revolver Ocelot as he appeared when first taken over by Liquid's psyche at the beginning of *MGS2*. The life bar name now reads "Liquid Ocelot," and again his persona and fighting style are a match. The encounter's final phase sees the face of a young Revolver Ocelot before he was taken over by Liquid flash across the screen and the name reads simply, "Ocelot."

---

[6]In this way, repetition as a tenet of play has clear implications for broader discussions on the limited, or perhaps unlimited, narrative structures found in video games. Damon Reece discusses some of the ways these structures might be explored through modular and systemic narratives.

He strikes his signature finger-gun pose at Snake before entering once more into battle.

Interestingly, during this last phase, Snake's name changes also to reflect the Snake that actually met Revolver Ocelot in 1964, the man Solid Snake is cloned from, "Naked Snake," as this fight plays out title music from each game in the series plays in succession, first from *MGS1*, then *MGS2*, and finally *MGS3*. Just as the bosses previous to this have been ghosts of bosses past, Liquid Ocelot's encounter serves as a nostalgic museum experience, as players are asked to consider the many Snakes that have squared off against Ocelot across the series.

> *Big Boss:* That's right. Good. No need for you to go just yet. It's been a long time... Snake.
>
> *Old Snake:* Big Boss?
>
> *Big Boss:* Let it go my son. I'm not here to fight. Or should I call you... brother?
>
> *Old Snake:* What?
>
> *Big Boss:* It's over, time for you to put aside the gun and live. It all began with a bunch of old fools. Now they've all passed away. Their era of folly is over. I'm the only one left, and soon I'll be gone too.
>
> *Old Snake:* How can you still be alive?
>
> *Big Boss:* That body Liquid burned on the Volta wasn't mine. That was the body of a clone—Solidus. He was a perfect clone. Zero, and the proxy AIs that came after him were convinced that Solidus was me. I was implanted with nanomachines, kept in a state of eternal sleep by JD the proxy AI. They had me sealed away completely. Not only my physical body but also my will too... For me to wake again, the system had to be destroyed one way or another. Ocelot and EVA wanted two things: to bring me back to life, and to end the Patriots... they put their grand scheme into motion. EVA stole my body from them and reconstructed it by replacing the missing parts with pieces from Liquid and Solidus. And Ocelot, in order to fool the system, used nanomachines and psychotherapy to transplant Liquid's personality onto his own. He used hypnotic suggestion to turn himself into Liquid's mental doppelganger. For all our advances in nanotechnology, information and genetic control they've never managed to control people

at will let alone turn one person totally into another. Under certain conditions, someone can be made to play a specific role, act like someone else. Cats do love to play as snakes.

(©Konami Digital Entertainment. With permission)

This concept of exhibiting a museum of past games is explored most explicitly in the "Déjà Vu" Extra Op of *MGSV:GZ*. This mission asks players to reflect on the history of the *Metal Gear* franchise as well as the studio and the enigma behind the series: Kojima Productions and its founder Hideo Kojima. It uses iteration to again close the distance between the player and the player-character.

The opening shot of "Déjà Vu" shows Snake kneeling on a rocky outcrop on the outskirts of Camp Omega, it's a familiar scene punctuated with a flashback to the opening menu screen of *MGS1*—"Press Start." All this followed by a familiar line uttered by many Snakes across the series: "Kept you waiting, huh?" As usual, Kazuhira Miller is the player's intel contact and he informs Snake that this mission is OSP (on-site procurement). Already this Extra Op is true to its name, intent on invoking the strangely familiar in *MGS3*'s Naked Snake. This was a codename given for the fact that Snake began his mission in the USSR without any gear, "naked," and procured all equipment on-site.

Miller continues: the challenge is to recreate seven scenes from the original *Metal Gear Solid* and then access the admin building inside the main compound. Intel photographs reveal each scene in need of recreation: a grounded helicopter with two guards stationed by it, Big Boss picking up an item on a helipad while avoiding searchlights, Big Boss driving a jeep, a guard being thrown from an exploding tank, a surveillance camera, a Moai statue, and finally a blank image. To this last intel photograph Miller comments, "Hm? The last photo's missing?...Oh, sorry... I forgot it. Snake, it should be on the back of the disc case. Or what about the manual? There's got to be a clue somewhere." Miller's instructions to check the disc case echo the same instructions given to Solid Snake by Arms Tech President Kenneth Baker in *MGS1* when he is attempting to contact Meryl Silverburgh via codec. Then, like now, the answer to the riddle is disguised as a promotional shot on the back cover, a black box with the word "HIDEO" in the top left corner. It's an image I instantly recognize and, sure enough, shutting down Camp Omega's power grid triggers an apparition of *MGS1*'s telepathic boss Psycho Mantis.

The numerous references throughout this mission to former Snakes, old bosses, viral weapons, cyborg ninjas, and soldiers with severe bowel problems are impossibly plentiful and equally as dense. Literally translated from the French for "already seen," *déjà vu* is the eerie feeling of having already experienced the present situation. As if recalled from a dream or shuffled from the back of the deck of your long-term memory, *déjà vu* gives pause for consideration: why tell the same story again and again and again? The answer, it seems, is because moments where the distance between Snake and the player is smallest are also moments of greatest narrative potential. Games tell stories that cannot be passively received; instead, they must be actively played and experienced through the body. The *Metal Gear* series' recognition of this distinction and its fervent desire to take both Snake and the player on a parallel narrative journey sets it apart.

Before completing the mission, players have the option of using their rifle's flashlight attachment to reveal *Metal Gear* series game logos emblazoned upon various walls, fences, and roofs across the compound. Finding the logos of the titles designated as canon by Hideo Kojima and sweeping across them with the flashlight will erase them. Erasing all game logos considered canon prompts Miller to remark that the memories of those games "will live on inside you." Additionally, an audio message from Kojima himself thanks players "for all [their] support." A year after *Ground Zeroes* release and Kojima Productions under Konami were disbanded and reformed as an independent studio. In this sense, "Déjà Vu" is a bittersweet farewell to the series. Even though *The Phantom Pain* was not yet released, it is apparent that the writing, quite literally, was on the wall.

Kojima's later installments to the franchise use iteration to amplify the role of the player. In the same way that engaging with limitation and identification closes the gap between Snake and the player, iteration proves to be a tenet of play leveraged for narrative power. Upon arrival at Shadow Moses island in *MGS1*, Snake opens with "This is Snake;" the series compels itself though to add a question mark to this phrase. If left simply as a statement, it provokes the question, which Snake? There's Solid Snake, Liquid Snake, Solidus Snake, Naked Snake, Punished Snake, Venom Snake, Old Snake and, of course, just Snake. Some of these codenames refer to the same person, or to genetically engineered clones, VR trained rookies, or even surgically altered body doubles under the illusion of hypnotherapy. This proliferation of Snakes serves to obfuscate the identity of any one Snake. The unifier of these codenames is none other than the player, each game proving itself to be a journey of becoming one Snake and erasing another. This is the journey of the player, over and over, to become Snake. Yet crucially players mustn't become just any Snake but their own version of Snake, forged by a play experience solely their own. As a series *Metal Gear* is an example of a narrative crafted uniquely and specifically for the player, about the player. The consistent narrowing of distance between Snake and the player at the moments when narrative and play intersect proves to be a unique storytelling tool. While it is true that these moments are often not exclusively narrative in nature, the narrative dividends awarded offer a glimpse at a type of game that is not necessarily at odds with its story. A symbiotic relationship between game design and narrative design emerges in the *Metal Gear* series: the quips of Psycho Mantis, the agency we experience through Raiden, the return of bosses we believed long dead, the kitsch merchandising of JF Rey sunglasses, all of it and much more is symptomatic of a series delivering not just a narrative or a game but both, at the same time, equally.

6

Interview with Anna Anthropy

Anna Anthropy is a game designer from the United States. In 2012, she released her critical hit, *Dys4ia*, and also published her first book, *Rise of the Videogame Zinesters*, showcasing the personal stories of a range of independent developers. She currently teaches game design at DePaul University College of Computing and Digital Media in Chicago.

Anna is determined to promote inclusivity and diversity in the industry and reflects on the toxic greed of big business in the online space in arguing that Triple-A games are hindered by a culture that continues to neglect marginalized voices. Her interest in hypertext, through programs such as Bisty and Twine, speaks to a long-term commitment to personal and nuanced human stories. We ask about her inspiration for using games as a means of creative self-expression and the importance of being able to see the author in the work. She explains the legacy of role-playing games for character and world-building and the power of oft-ignored narrative tools, such as failure, to be as effective as technology in advancing storytelling in the medium. She believes that the future of games writing lies in social interaction, accessible technology, and the democratization of gamer culture.

Timothy Williams: You make such varied and bold games, Anna. What sort of games do you play? What kinds of stories and experiences in games do you find the most engaging?

Anna Anthropy: These days what I'm playing mostly is games made with the Bitsy tool. That's for a few reasons. One is that I don't usually have the time to play things that are longer than an hour or so, and the other main reason is that I'm a teacher, which means that I'm constantly on the lookout for incredibly short games that I can shoehorn into my classes. I haven't dug around in Bitsy and made anything in it yet, but I'm really impressed with a lot of the narrative space that's being explored by creators. There's not a lot of ways to do really involved systems designing a Bitsy game, and so creators have to explore narrative and storytelling in a really interesting spatial way. Those are the only games that'll pop up on my Twitter feed, and I'll just go, "oh, I can probably play this right now."

EP: What are the ingredients of a spatial narrative? What does that involve and what are the types of narrative can it produce?

AA: What's really interesting to me about Bitsy games is that it's often hard to have strict control over the way the player encounters scenes or moments in the plot. It's almost as though the narrative becomes a texture that the player brushes their hand over. There's not a lot of the authorial control that we usually find in traditional games. It's more akin to reading a book, where there is the feeling that the pace of the experience and the rhythm of it are ultimately up to the player, and nothing moves forward without them. There's room to linger and to play out the story very slowly and hang out and really engage with spaces and interrogate them. Or you can hurdle forward through scene transitions and whatnot. That makes it really interesting to me because digital games so often, especially games that we think of as narrative driven games—something like a Telltale game—have an almost relentless pace that's very much refereed by the creators and that's enforced by the game's systems. Things happen at a constant speed; events unfold at a rate dictated by the authors. In Bitsy, it's a little messier; it's a little more open in a way that I find really interesting and also really nonpressuring.

EP: So rather than plot being reinforced by the system, you have a slightly more ambient experience? That's what it sounds like to me.

AA: Yeah, kind of like that. Also, there's almost the feeling of turning the page. There's this idea that events and scenes won't move forward until you decide that they're going to move forward. So there's a different relationship between the game and the viewer than I think there is in a lot of digital games. It's kind of more comfortable, but also it's really interesting that it feels like power is more shared between the author and the audience in those games.

TW: It's interesting you talk about authorial control. Do you think that a position like the auteur is even applicable to games?

AA: I think games have a little too many auteurs. We could do with fewer of those. The other thing that's really interesting to me about things like Bitsy or Twine, game making tools that are relatively systems-lite, and free, and more accessible, is that the people who come to game authorship through them are not auteurs. It's people who are coming from marginalized perspectives but whose approaches to storytelling are often more fragmented and fractured. It's more like a zine-ing or journaling experience. There's an element of vulnerability that comes into play when people are writing close to their chests, which I think to me is very different from the auteur kind of approach to development.

TM: So is that where most of the inspiration in your own work comes from? Your own experiences? Or do you try and meter that out—a little bit from your own experiences but also from other fiction?

AA: I don't think there's much to be gained from trying to erase the author from the work. My work is definitely informed by my life, especially in the sense that I'm going to write what's interesting to me and what I know, which are very much informed by my own experiences. I think that kind of writing is both more honest and generally more interesting. I'm not really interested in playing the same stories, the same kind of games again and again. I'm really interested in what the voices that traditionally do not have a lot of representation in games have to say. I want to know what people on the fringes of society, and also the fringes of game development, have to say. Traditional routes into game development privilege really normative kinds of people. Marginalized people are just not going to be able to afford the training, but they're also going to get filtered out by the culture, harassed off of the Internet. And so for a lot of people for whom these sorts of traditional channels aren't open, things like hypertext[1] can open a route into game development that previously didn't exist. And those works that those people are making are going to be informative experiences. That to me is way more exciting.

EP: It's fascinating to hear these ideas—fractured approaches to narrative, more fragmented approaches to storytelling. And drawing on life experience, having that as part of the texture of games, that's really interesting.

AA: I was participating in an online Twitter chat the other day about queerness as it pertains to digital texts, and especially the hypertexts, and one of the things I said was that I feel like hypertext—things like Twine and Bitsy—lend really well to more liminal experiences and liminal identities, because they are so fragmented. I think the nature of hypertext fiction lends itself really well to voices that are in conflict with themselves, that have a lot of complexity, and that aren't neat and tidy. I think that's why a lot of work from marginalized voices from outsiders is so interesting, because in many cases it's less filtered, more vulnerable, more self-critical, and engaged in interesting conversations within itself. And because of that, it's using the format in ways that more singular voices are not, and that makes for a lot of really interesting narrative exploration of what an interactive or nonlinear narrative could even look like.

WC: Could these sorts of voices come through in the Triple-A space? Have you ever thought about what a big budget

---

[1] "Hypertexts" are any texts that are not constrained by the linearities of traditional writing. Hypertext games usually involve a combination of links to other texts, graphics, or audio, with which the player can interact.

Anna Anthropy game might be? Or are there too many limitations in that form?

AA: I would love to have the time and resources to hire people to work on something that was a long-form project. I cannot see myself working on something on the scale of, for example, *Red Dead Redemption*, because I think that model of game making is unsustainable. A lot of my projects were developed very quickly, because for the longest time, I was basically on the verge of poverty while I was developing games. And if I spent too long on a project, I might not make rent that month, so I developed a process of working on very quick and small projects, spending a week on them, and then calling them done. So it would be exciting to have the luxury of just being able to spend time endlessly tweaking and doing iterative development, and just comfortably working on a project. It would probably result in things that are very structurally different than a lot of the stuff I've made. One of my most celebrated interactive fiction games is a game that literally takes 10 s to play.[2] And that's the product definitely of this wild, accelerated development cycle that doesn't leave a lot of room for going back and polishing and smoothing out the edges. But, generally, that's what I think makes games interesting to me—the messiness, the edges where you actually see the author a little bit more than you would in something where all the corners have been rounded off, you know?

EP: Yeah, absolutely. I wanted to follow up on Will's question, actually, and turn away from those really problematic productions models of the Triple-A space and instead consider the dimension of scope and duration of a game. You were saying your daily experience, and it's very similar to mine, is that there's no time to play a game with a longer duration. I'm interested in games where some of those storytelling techniques that are more established in the independent space—things like fragmentation and fracturing and playing with authorial voice—have

---

[2] *Queers in Love at the End of the World* (2013).

translated across to games with a longer duration. Can you think of examples that have touched you in any way?

AA: Oh, boy, this is where I have to actually remember what games I've played recently. Geez…

EP: You can use it as a thought experiment, even if you just wanted to play with those ingredients. Can you think about how scope and duration might also be a texture in independent storytelling?

AA: I've played a game by Michael Brough that took literally 6 months to play through. It's called *Vesper.5*. It's a pretty basic game. Whenever you play, you get to make a single move—up, down, left, or right. It's like a pilgrim's journey. The person who you're moving is dressed in monk vestments, and there are some ambient little bells and chimes playing. You can only make one of those moves, one space per day, and then you have to come back the next day. Every time when you log in, it plays out your entire journey up to the present moment, and then you get to make another move, and it takes months to get through the entire game, and that's interesting to me. It was created for a game jam,[3] and the theme was "ritual," and the idea is that it's a game that you have to make a daily ritual. You literally have to fit it into your daily schedule somewhere regular if you want to make it through the game. That to me is the interesting possibility of longer form games—the possibility of ritual and of a tradition to build up around it, almost to the point of introducing a myth to the game. By the time I saw the ending, there was so much narrative weight that I'd put onto what is essentially a really simple and really nondescript game. What's interesting to me about longer form games is not the fact that they provide more content or whatever, but the idea that they can explore avenues of experience that you can only really explore with a lot of time. Something like *The Sims* is close to this, the idea of really being able to sit with things and return to things over a long period,

---

[3]A "game jam" is a gathering of game designers in which the goal is to produce one or more games within a short time span—usually no more than a few days.

which is not the way we usually experience longer form games. Games like *Red Dead Redemption*—most players are going to spend their time with the game in long marathon sessions, rather than playing like 10 min every day. I'm not interested in the scale as much as I'm interested in the relationship to time and how that could be different.

EP: It brings to mind these other ingredients that are perhaps more theatrical. My background and training is in live art and performance art, and there's that aspect of ritual that I connect with, which is not perhaps typically found in a game that's developed around a more screenwriting kind of model.

AA: It's really interesting. I think there's a lot of aspects of performance and play that I think are undersold. It's a space that's underexplored in digital games. It feels almost more natural in physical games, like tabletop games.

TW: Can you speak a bit about failure in games, and how it might be linked to other aspects, like progress, challenge, and pacing?

AA: I think that failure is really interesting, but a lot of games don't make it interesting. We have a really narrow idea of progress, and that includes progress in a story, and that it's always tied to success. Failure means that we have to go back and try again. Failure means the story does not continue to unfold. The game will come to a halt until we have achieved whatever's necessary to move forward. My own design practice today is way more in tabletop role-playing games than it is in digital games anymore, and one of the reasons that I've been drawn into that space is that there is a lot more interesting space to explore failure and to use failure as a way of moving the story forward and finding narrative momentum. Traditionally, in a *Dungeons and Dragons*-style game, if you roll the dice well, that means you do the thing, and if you roll poorly, that means you don't do the thing. In *Apocalypse World*, which is a seminal indie role-playing game—it basically inspired hundreds of other games—success means you get something you wanted, but that maybe there's a hidden cost. Failure means that even though you didn't quite get to do the thing you wanted, something else will still happen. In digital games especially, we just ignore the potential for failure to be narratively interesting, for it to snowball into other narrative moments and possibilities. I think one of the reasons is that there's a level of budget at which point failure is economically unfeasible to explore. If you think about something like *Red Dead Redemption*, the budget of that game and the amount of labor that's going into it, having something happen when you fail in addition to when you succeed, that's more content which costs more, whereas interestingly, in spaces where content is cheaper, like in Twine games and in Bitsy games, I think there's more room to explore what failure can mean and not just what success looks like. Not just to have the one narrative that moves forward when you do the thing, but also to have narratives that go in a lot of different directions and use failure in interesting ways. I think role-playing games are the best at this because all of the content is user-supplied, but I think there's room absolutely for traditional games to explore meanings of failure beyond, "you messed up. Do it again."

EP: So you're imagining a space where not every narrative moment is a training moment? It could be a more creative, emergent moment?

AA: Often, failures are character moments. You know, failure is an opportunity to highlight the limitations and challenges of a character in the story. So it's sad to see that underused. One of the things that I have my students play in the games theory class that I teach is a role-playing game called *Firebrands*, by Vincent Baker. It's a mech anime about pilots falling in love with their most hated enemies. And one of the imperatives that I put on my students when I send them out to play this game is that you will probably want to put your character in situations where they win and where they're doing things that they're good at. You're probably going to set them up to succeed. But you will get the most interesting story if you put them in places where they will fail. If you put your characters in situations where they are caught off guard, where they are not playing to their strengths. That is where you will find the most interesting character moments, where you will create the most interesting tangled stories. A lot of our ideas of what a character is in a game come from something like *Dungeons and Dragons*, where the whole system of character advancement is set up so that if you want your character to do well, you need to always make sure that they are doing the thing that they're best at and doing as little as possible of things that they're not good at. That's how you get rewarded and that's how you get experience points, which leads to really shallow explorations of character, because we're never getting the opportunities to put our characters in situations where they're challenged or weak. There are a lot of opportunities for weakness in games storytelling that we're not exploiting.

TW: Why, historically, do you think that's been the case? Does it speak to the male power fantasy? Many gamers don't really want to fail.

AA: Yeah, there's a weird pampering that goes on in games, where I think that players are sincerely challenged by the notion of fallibility. A lot of players have been trained to feel very threatened by that idea. Games are marketed as spaces that are empowering, often to people who are actually very empowered already in their day-to-day lives. The idea of engaging in an experience that is going to be disempowering is very challenging. The irony of that is that I think the people who are most scared of that are the people who are the most in power in their day-to-day lives. That's a potent fear, and fascism in the US is built on the myth that the most powerful are actually the victims. Fear has a lot of power, and gamers have not been challenged enough on that front yet.

WC: I'm interested in what led you to the space you're in now, Anna. As a kid, did you always have personal stories you wanted to tell? Or was it a case of being dragged into games by other people's stories before finding your own voice?

AA: As a kid, a lot of the games I made were incredibly derivative because that's what you make when you first start making games. When I was around 9 or 10, I discovered a free fairly accessible game-making tool called

ZZT, which I have a whole book on the subject of. The first game stories that I told were very much modeled off games I was familiar with and stories that I was familiar with. I tried to minimize my fingerprints on it in a lot of ways, and, as a result, when I grew up to adulthood, I grew out of games for a while because they didn't feel relevant to the person I was becoming. They didn't seem like they really spoke to what my life was or my identity. So I did go through a phase where I quit games for a long time because they just didn't seem relevant to my life. Then, when I got back into it, when I started discovering new tools like Game Maker, my first thought was, "I have so much to tell about the experience of being a person like me." When I got back into making games as an adult, I was very much of the opinion that queer perspectives aren't really represented very well in games, especially queer women's perspectives. So that was a driving force behind a lot of the indie game work I was doing. I wanted to tell stories about people who have experiences like me, because those stories are not getting told and we can't rely on the games industry to tell them.

TW: Have you noticed a change since you got back into making games as an adult? Do you think the terms "game designer" and "game developer" are undergoing a transition? Are they perhaps being democratized and now encompassing a wider group of people?

AA: Yes and no. One of the things the game industry has realized is that they can weaponize gamers—as in people who identify as gamers and consider themselves to be loyal to the publishers of the brands. They can weaponize those people to maintain the status quo. If you look at something like Gamergate,[4] which was a thing I lived through and was targeted in, along with a lot of people I cared about, you can see the way those groups of people were very loyal to a certain idea of game design. They were exploited to push marginalized people back out of gaming, specifically

---

[4]"Gamergate" refers to a controversy surrounding the harassment of prominent female figures in the video game industry.

out of game development and game authorship. I don't think the industry has quite moved past that. I don't think a lot of people have really even acknowledged the effect that Gamergate had on the industry and the way that it pushed out a lot of marginalized people. That doesn't mean that the metamorphosis still isn't happening, but I think a lot of the people who were the most involved in creating that change were forced out. So it's weird—it hasn't stopped the amount of people who are making weird interesting little games because I don't think that trend can be stopped. I think the diversification of voices that's going on, and what it means to make games, it's like the tide—it has to happen—but I haven't seen it is happening without violent repercussions for the people who are the most vulnerable and the most involved in enacting that change. There's a big discussion about unions in the game industry right now and actually stepping up to safeguard the rights of game developers. That's another struggle. It will happen, but I don't see it is happening without a lot of people being hurt. Maybe that's a pessimistic view, and obviously, I want to be hopeful, but I think that the games industry is really resistant to change. Gamers have bought into a myth about games and who is providing them and who can take them away. I don't think it's very conducive to meaningful change, and it sucks for the people who are the most vulnerable and it sucks for the people who are on the front lines of making change.

EP: That's really interesting, Anna, and it provides a nice platform for us to turn from that cultural view, that wider view, into the more specific storytelling ingredients of games. With the people, we've been speaking to, for this book, it tends to go in two directions. Some return to the essence of story ingredients and think that's in some ways where the future of games lies—going back to those simple stories and exploring them in more interesting ways. Then we have the other side of that—the promise of new technology, whether VR or other kinds of immersive technologies, and how those will help to shape new story possibilities. What do you see as some of the futures here?

AA: I'm very interested in exploding storytelling and our existing forms. I not only think that, obviously, things like VR can afford new possibilities, but I also think that a lot of the technologies that are enabling, and are going to enable, the most interesting new forms of storytelling are not necessarily cutting-edge technologies. I think a lot of them are probably social technologies. You look at something like Twine and the really interesting exploration of hypertext storytelling that it enables. Twine is something that could have been made years ago. It's not an amazing, cutting-edge top of the line technology. I think the technology it brought and enabled was access, and the ability to couple writing really closely with interactivity. Those are not technologies that are very expensive, but I think they are all the social technologies, the human technologies, which the games industry is way more deficient in. That is what is going to bring the most interesting, newest, wildest, and most revolutionary forms of storytelling. A lot of it is putting tools in the hands of people who have new forms of stories and new formats of stories to explore and tell. Twine has allowed for the creation of new and more interesting interactive forms of storytelling because it has enabled different voices to tell different stories in different ways. Ultimately, one of the things that is going to transform storytelling in games is developing not just the machines that we use but also developing a vocabulary for exploring the social in games, exploring relationships in games, exploring the kind of oft-invisible nuances of how human beings relate to each other, and getting into how we think about, model, and explore that, using interactivity. That's what I think is going to lead to more interesting storytelling futures. Not just that you have a headset that you can put on and move your neck around. Sure, the headset is going to add something, but there is so much out there that is just uncharted because we haven't been putting the energy into charting out the nuance of it, and I hope we do.

7

New Horizons
Open Worlds and Storyfeel

I am two-thirds of the way through Guerilla Games' *Horizon Zero Dawn* (2017). I have been playing for 56 hours, and I'm fairly sure I may never finish all of the tasks, side quests, and interludes that are included in this adventure-fantasy world. The central character of *Horizon* is Aloy, a young huntress armed with various bows, slings, traps, and a spear, and I have spent more time with Aloy than I have with almost any other fictional character in all of the books, TV series, movies, live performances, and games I have previously consumed.[1] Aloy is fairly charismatic, and her writers and designers evoke a sense of humor and sass, but this is not why I'm spending these hours. It's more that epic game environments like *Horizon* are expanding the range of narrative interactions and building vast worlds wherein a commitment of a 7-day working week feels more like a comma than the end of a sentence.

In this chapter, I'm going to examine the Triple-A title *Horizon Zero Dawn* alongside another game from 2016, *The Witness*, a puzzle-game by well-known independent game designer Jonathan Blow. I want to explore how creative writers for games are playing with narrative techniques, ludic immersion, and environmental storytelling to enhance the experience of games. Whereas in previous chapters, Will and Tim have drawn attention to the increasing sophistication of creative writing in games in the interactions between story, narrative, and the role of the player, this chapter will highlight how the experience of contemporary games is also deeply connected to the environment, both built and imagined, in the game world. Specifically, I will argue that one of the fundamental innovations in recent creative writing for

---

[1] See Keogh's comments on labor, time, and player attachment in Chapter 4.

games is the degree to which "open-world" games allow for new storytelling techniques and interactions that are as much about the accumulation of experiences (both banal and battle-driven) than they are about narrative conclusion.

On returning to gaming after 15 years, one of the most profound changes I've noticed is the degree to which world building and storytelling techniques have radically expanded. My first console was a Sega Mega Drive. I had played games on an Atari 2600 and Nintendo, but the Mega Drive was really the start of my interactions and obsessions with games. Though, I almost never played alone. Games were a thing to do with my younger brother and sister, and our friends, which meant the experience was always about negotiation, commentary, and competitiveness. And moving! While our parents may have complained about us staring at a screen, one of my most profound memories of playing video games as a child is that I was often moving; clutching the controller, jabbing at the buttons, and jumping to my feet when I was facing a difficult section or getting close to finishing a level. Brendan Keogh, interviewed for this volume, writes evocatively of a phenomenology of video game experience as a "play of bodies," by which he means the interactions between virtual and physical sensations and worlds. For Keogh, video games are touched, seen, heard, and understood through our bodies—not only that, video games touch us back (2018: 6). I felt this clash of sensations whenever Sonic was bouncing through the Casino Night Zone in *Sonic the Hedgehog 2* (1992). I felt I was only ever partly in control. I was seeing, hearing, and perceiving through the experience of playing, and I guess many of the games I played then prioritized speed and a certain type of adrenaline-fueled perception over a multilayered story. Levels and endings were a common experience, but while sometimes there was a narrative attached to this movement— Sonic's serial harassment of Doctor Eggman, for example—the narrative always tended to act as a background element to the gameplay mechanics, graphics, and the bossfight. While these elements remain integral to an overwhelming number of game designs and scenarios (whether they are linear in progression or more free-roaming), I am continually surprised at the extent to which exploration in an expansive environment serves to deepen my engagement with the game world. In this sense, the narrative potentials arising from the story world don't seem to be background elements anymore but have become increasingly intermingled in dynamic interaction with both the gameplay and the environment of the game: in many ways, world-building equals story-building.

Narrative Design in the Post-Post-Apocalypse

Horizon Zero Dawn, released by publisher Sony Interactive Entertainment in February 2017, is currently one of the best-selling PlayStation 4 games of all time, with more than 7 million copies sold by February 2018. It is also a representative example of single-player open-world games, for its emphasis on the "free" movement of the player/character within a virtual game world. As Richard Moss argues, open-world games constitute a genre that has existed since the 1970s, which makes freedom—you, the player, can *decide* what to do next—a central element of the game design (2017). Paradigmatic examples of this genre as it has developed in 21st century gaming include *Grand Theft Auto III* (2001), *Assassin's Creed* (2007), *Red Dead Redemption* (2010), and now *Red Dead Redemption 2* (2018). Open worlds also include the subgenre of the action-RPG such as *Horizon* and other more recent offerings like *The Witcher 3: Wild Hunt* (2015) and *Middle-earth: Shadow of War* (2017). These games typically contain a main storyline or central quest as well as other sandbox elements such as side quests, puzzles, skill challenges, and in-game interactions with a variety of characters. As such, contemporary RPGs often combine a branching narrative structure—in which completed quests open up new story elements—with tasks that can be completed in any order in a more modular fashion (Heussner et al., 2015: 111–121). There is the potential then, for nonlinear movement within a game world that nonetheless contains linear stories and a central narrative.

In *Horizon*, the main character is an outcast from a tribe of hunter-gatherer humans. After an opening credits sequence, an extended nonplayable scene, which sees a baby (Aloy) being taken through the various landscapes of *Horizon* to her naming ceremony, carried by her father figure Rost.

> Today I speak your name, girl. But—will the Goddess speak it back ... we are outcasts. Even so, we keep the tribes rituals. Otherwise we might become like the faithless Old Ones, who turned their backs on the Goddess. But their wickedness doomed them. To us were left the splendors of creation...

Following the naming ceremony, attended by a pair of squabbling Matriarchs, the action jumps forward 6 years to reveal Aloy as a lonely child who is not allowed to participate in tribal life.

At the beginning of any game, a number of crucial elements are constructed, in particular the rules of the game world need to be established, and the player needs to learn the mechanics of the gameplay. With this in mind, games commonly begin with sort variety of tutorial section. After Aloy falls into a cave, the playable moments begin, and I spend the first portion of the game learning the basic mechanics (crouch, run, dash, jump, etc.). I also get more of a glimpse into backstory of the character and her world, a kind of postapocalyptic Earth in which tribes of humans who have survived a world-ending disaster live in conflict with a range of robotic creatures. In the cave, I inspect a futuristic device, a triangular metal chip, which enables Aloy to "Focus" and scan her surrounding environment to locate hidden puzzle mechanics and information. As I move deeper into the cave, I uncover ruins of a technologically sophisticated society and the remains of several bodies—some of which can be scanned to reveal audio testimonies and texts from the past that further build backstory and context for the action to come. Indeed, from the early moments of *Horizon*, the writers and designers carefully interlink in-game discoveries and stories with the backstory narrative for the world, and the character of Aloy herself.

Following her exit from the cave ruins, Rost starts to train Aloy/me to hunt the robot creatures, and I learn the second layer of game mechanics, the combat, gathering, inventory, and stealth features of the game. I collect some medicinal berries and start moving more freely through a woodland, with pine trees and grasses. Throughout these moments, Rost is moving ahead and delivering a constant stream of information and instructions, as when we see the first machine called a Watcher—a Velociraptor-like robot with a huge glowing eye. "You must learn to avoid their gaze if you want to survive," says Rost. The creatures frequently resemble mechanical dinosaurs—I couldn't help but imagine some of them transforming like a Dinobot—and the initial landscape Aloy moves through also recalls the lush plains of *Jurassic Park* (1993). The final moments of the training sequence presents me with a challenge—to use all of the elements of gameplay learnt so far to rescue a tribe member who is surrounded by robots (Figure 7.1).

> *Rost:* I can do nothing. It's only a matter of time before the machines find that boy and kick him to death. But if I shoot, it will cause a stampede, and it will trample him.
>
> *Aloy uses her Focus to scan the environment and sees the patrol patterns of the creatures.*
>
> *Aloy:* But I can see the paths they take!
>
> *Rost:* Stop telling stories.

FIGURE 7.1
Horizon Zero Dawn

(a)

(b)

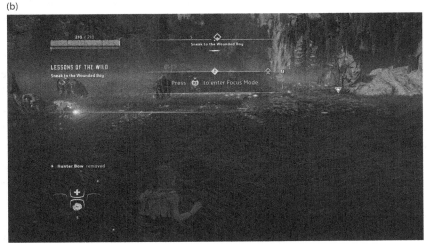

(a) Tutorial with Aloy and Rost
(b) A Lesson in process

This small tutorial section alone combines the cutscene above, establishing Aloy's principled and impetuous personality, and encourages me to then apply the basic mechanics of the gameplay within a story scene. Yet, alongside this basic structure (cut scene followed by playable challenge), the prologue section of *Horizon*, which takes roughly 30 min, also profiles a range of other narrative devices that are used throughout the rest of the game. The ambition of the narrative design is immediately evident: there is in-game dialogue between Aloy, Rost, and other members of the Nora tribe; several cutscenes in which characters engage in dialogue; expository text in the form of documents and audio files found in the underground ruin; "flashpoint" moments in which Aloy is challenged and asked to choose from three possible reactions (confrontation, insight, or compassion), task-based narration in the form of gameplay and training tips—how to sneak up on a mechanical creature or use combat skills and so on—that also acts as a form of exposition about the world; and, finally, there is a degree of "free" exploration in which Aloy can negotiate the landscape, gathering herbs, flowers, and collectables, as well as tackling steep terrain through climbing and parkour. The various narrative devices found in the prologue act as a template for how the world-building possibilities of *Horizon* may be used as the catalyst for character and story development. For Guerilla Games' Narrative Director John Gonzales: "Everything about the ancient world … [it's] directly related to Aloy's story. It turns out that the riddle of her birth and her origins is essentially the riddle of how this world came to be (2018)." In short, as Aloy learns about her world, how to hunt, gather, and hide, and how she came to be an outcast, the player learns alongside her.

In many ways, contemporary Triple-A games like *Horizon Zero Dawn* are not made for me. Firstly, I have limited time to play them, an hour here and there between the commitments of family, work, sleep, and (god forbid) exercise. Second, I find linear game narratives, cutscenes, and in-game dialogues are often poorly scripted and lack development—meaning that once I have learnt the game mechanics and leveled up to the point when I can face most challenges, there is little incentive to continue playing. Indeed, as Moss notes, while the vast majority of all commercial games are now set in open worlds, this is no guarantee of quality (2017), with many open-world maps simply being cluttered with endless minimarkers for tasks and side quests that are of little consequence to the game world.[2] What is left then, are not the narratives in and of themselves, but how all of the story potentials of the game might intersect with the world-building project of the designers. As Narrative Director John Gonzalez states:

---

[2] More than a few of these tasks are brutally repetitive: I'm looking at you, tank bits in *Batman: Arkam Knight* (2016); frustrating and repetitive, see the central mechanic of *No Man's Sky* (2017); or downright exploitative, as in pretty much any game requiring cash for credits.

We were trying to create a hybrid between … a massive open-world role-playing game in terms of the scope of the world and also the depth of the lore, and a lot of the pleasures of interactive dialogue and with some choice, but we were really trying to blend that with … an action adventure that has an authored character, that has a defined arc, and the cinematic storytelling that is used to convey that.

(No Clip, 2018)

As Gonzalez signals, *Horizon* is an example of an open-world game in which linear narrative techniques are cleverly interwoven into the more exploratory gameplay. The opening prologue is indicative of this approach because even though there are explicit cutscenes and in-game dialogues, I also learn about the world and the game mechanics by interacting with the environment.

When he was brought into work on *Horizon*, Gonzalez notes that Guerilla had already come up with a strong concept of the world—tribes of humans living in beautiful post-postapocalypic nature alongside robotic dinosaurs, and featuring a tough young machine-hunter—but that the studio acknowledged that the ambition of the world needed to be supported by an equally ambitious approach to storytelling. Guerilla formed an internal writing team, and Gonzalez recruited writers to try and stitch together the previously developed elements of the game, such as the concept of the world, and existing lore and character backstories, into a script that contained a curated story with a clear narrative arc and a more developed central character. For Gonzalez, the "rare" experience of being in a creative environment in which writing is considered of paramount importance to the game design was one of the defining features of working on *Horizon* (2018). The writing team worked initially to weave together two interconnected elements: the backstory of the world, what happened to the ancient civilization? And the backstory of Aloy, who is she and what is driving her? In the words of Gonzalez: "The ambition was to create an experience that is both highly personal and hugely epic" and where the answers to the key questions are embedded in the journey of Aloy throughout the game as she uncovers more of her past (2018).

As reviewer Zoe Delanhunty-Light notes, the intricacies of the world are connected to this experience of discovery.

Like a real ecosystem, *Horizon: Zero Dawn* is brilliantly balanced. Aloy feels like an inextricable part of it, halfway between prey and predator. Whether you're climbing cliff-faces with a weightless, fluid joy, hunting, or travelling through the landscape, *Horizon: Zero Dawn* takes you on a tour of discovery. An endless sense of wonder and awe push you onward no matter what you're doing. The more time I spend in *Horizon: Zero Dawn's* world, the less I want to leave.

(2017)

As Delanhunty-Light's review points out, the-player-as-Aloy begins to piece together the story of her world not only through the various linear narrative sequences but also through her *experience of being in the world.* Similarly, one of the reasons I retain interest in games like *Horizon* is due to the moments of nonlinear discovery in which the game world provokes connections between story, character, and play in a way that "feels" organic. As such, my reading of *Horizon* is now going to move away from any analysis of cutscenes. As a player, I'm not hugely interested in having a narrative explicitly spelt-out for me. Rather, I want to concentrate on the moments when the open elements of the game design provoke additional creative and playful engagements with the game world, where the experience of story is disconnected from a narrative engine that overwhelmingly relies on traditional devices like a linear plot.

Indeed, after I complete the early quests and training modules, the game-world map begins to expand. This map, which is revealed gradually by moving through it or opening up large sections by finding giraffe-like creatures called Tallnecks, is immense and contains regions of grasslands, woodlands, jungles, deserts, and snowy mountains. As I move through the different terrain, I discover and hunt various machines, as the main narrative reveals Aloy's past and the origin story of the creatures. But increasingly, I also get distracted and undertake various side quests, gain skills in order to level up, search for collectable items on the sides of mountains, atop ruined skyscrapers and in underground bunkers, and engage in random wandering. *Horizon* resembles other open-world games that frequently contain moments when you are simply negotiating the environment, on foot, in a vehicle or, in this case on the back of a mechanical horse.[3] Wandering in a game like *Horizon* is, for me, one of the unique aspects of the video game experience. As a player, I often prefer scavenging and roaming more than focusing on completing a quest. This is not because I don't enjoy the puzzles or battles, but because I enjoy more that when I am given the illusion of freedom within a game world I tend to start engaging with the story in a different way.

---

[3] When Tim plays *Horizon*, he avoids riding or fast travel in favor of running. "Why would I ride a horse when everything is so beautiful to look at?" he says.

Relatively early in the game I am negotiating a place called Devil's Thirst and heading toward a nearby Vantage point. I've found earlier that Vantages are places to climb, but up until this point, I haven't really taken much notice of them. I'm not entirely sure how to find it, but in a landscape of green slopes and red grasses, I find the hulking remains of what might have been a city center. It's like a scrapyard for skyscrapers, which is now overgrown by plants, with trees twining through a mess of steel remains. In the background, I can hear, and feel through the controller, the thudding footsteps of a Tallneck. I start climbing one of the buildings, following a path of yellow climbing holds. Sometimes, they are difficult to locate, but when I do, Aloy can easily leap and clamber up the ruin. At the top, I am far above the treetops and can look over to a mountain range that is looming close by. On the ledge, I find a message that can be accessed through using my Focus. I open it, and the image of a modern city flashes up next to my ear like a thought bubble. It is the image of the environment as it used to be. I listen to the audio log (Figure 7.2):

> Bashar Mati: Apocashitstorm Tour, day 4. It's hard to believe Metallurgic International used to be headquartered in this dreary old ziggurat. Wyatt's office was on the second floor from the top. If M. Int had a policy against workplace romances, he probably wrote it.

FIGURE 7.2
Horizon Zero Dawn

Colorado Springs Vantage Point.

Other than the brief bit of Lore from the audio log, there are no other instructions, and when I turn the Focus off, the image disappears. Nonetheless, I recognize the glimpse of the past, a moment of exposition that is thoroughly enmeshed with the gameplay and a moment when my experience of the world, and identification with the character of Aloy, deepens. In these sections, I feel as though I am half-lost in the game world, not heading anywhere in particular, and simply "stumble" upon or climb up into, a ruin. Yet the use of Vantage points—there are 12 of them in all—is one way the game manages to unite story world and game world without the use of nonplayable cutscenes, explicit instructions, or other linear narrative devices.

Moments like the Vantage Points are largely contingent on in-game choices and exploration. While they are part of a challenge to complete all 12 and could be undertaken in a linear fashion with an enclosed narrative, they also offer ways to interact with and become immersed in the various story potentials and nonlinear narratives that arise from the game world. I would suggest that these potentials exist in conjunction with explicit environmental storytelling—in which story elements are communicated through the environmental design of a game—but I would argue that a key to developing unique game stories is when environmental storytelling features begin to augment and overlap with the experience of world-building and the overarching narrative design of the game. This is particularly evident in *Horizon* when the movement of the game-character responds to the physical movements of the player, the movement of Aloy as she climbs, which starts to intermingle with the other story elements of the game. As Steve Swink argues, "gamefeel" includes the design of the physical controller and how the game responds to the physical inputs of the player mashing the buttons, but also narrative and contextual elements, along with the graphics, sound, and musical score (2009). It is no surprise, then, that Gonzalez also speaks about the ambition of Guerilla Games to design a game that was "something that is beautiful in every dimension;" beautiful not only in terms of look and play but also in terms of the story (2018). With this in mind, the fluid way in which Aloy navigates the ruin, the responsiveness of the game engine to my own movements, the stunning view across to the mountains, and the distant thudding sound of the Tallneck, all add a dimension to my experience of the hologrammatic image of the past: because the game *feels* cohesive, so does my experience of the story at that moment. This is different to understanding a narrative as logical or that an environment helps reveal the story, and more about how the *gamefeel* is connected to when writing and designing for games intermingles these elements in the overall narrative design of the story world. We might call this aspect of game design the *storyfeel*, and for an idea of how storyfeel can also exist without any semblance of linear narrative devices, I now turn to game "without" a story—Jonathan Blow's *The Witness*.

Story-Riddles in *The Witness*

The Witness was released by Blow's own independent company Thekla Inc. in January 2016. It is a first-person puzzle game, in which the player explores an island with 11 different regions in order to solve approximately 650 puzzles. As distinct from *Horizon Zero Dawn*, *The Witness* is not a Triple-A blockbuster in terms of marketing and budget and is without the support of a major publisher. Nevertheless, with 7 years in development, the game is close to a Triple-A game in its scope and polish (Conditt, 2016). Drawing on the example of *Myst* (1993), a groundbreaking puzzle game that was also a first-person adventure story set on an island, *The Witness* strips away narrative devices such as cutscenes and dialogue to focus primarily on nonverbal game elements.

The game begins in a dark tunnel. The space is lit at the far end by a yellow square, mounted into a circular door, and the walls are gray and smooth. The player/me moves toward the door, and as I reach it, I can see that the square has a horizontal line through it with a small circle at one end, not unlike the shape of a keyhole laid on its side. I engage with the square, the first puzzle, by moving a cursor dot onto the small circle, clicking, and then following the horizontal line with the cursor. Once I have successfully drawn the line and clicked again, the door opens. This basic mechanic, the dot and then the drawing of a line, and the subtle sound cues that accompany the task, is used throughout the rest of the game, and I have just completed the most important tutorial of the game in the first 5 s of play. After moving through the first door, I arrive in a dark space, and see another puzzle square in another door, this time mounted into a rock wall. This puzzle has a single line with a small circle at one end, only this time the line has a 90° turn in the middle. As before, I move the cursor to the circle and trace the line to the end to unlock the door. It opens to reveal a corridor leading up to a glimpse of blue sky in the distance, and I move toward the outside world. As Blow has remarked, "Triple-A games tend to be heavily tutorialized at the beginning … and it makes a lot of these games tedious (2008)." In contrast, *The Witness* focuses on a very simple mechanic and then expands on this initial idea for the rest of the game. As this opening demonstrates, while the basic mechanic remains the same, each puzzle is different, and once you have learnt one element or rule, the game challenges you to learn a slightly different element and solve increasingly difficult puzzles.

Following my exit from the tunnel, I emerge into a walled courtyard, a space that looks like the ruins of a small castle, overgrown with lush grass, rocks, and trees, and a purple flowering wisteria clinging to the far wall. The colors are bright and slightly saturated and, similar to the regions of *Horizon*, the landscapes of *The Witness* island range from jungle areas to woods and desert. Both games invite the player to explore these environments, both are full of grand ruins and deserted buildings, but whereas *Horizon* uses its opening scenes to give backstory and context to the postapocalyptic story world and the main character (as befits an action-RPG), in *The Witness* there is a notable absence of overt narrative elements. There are no cutscenes or in-game dialogues, and while the game has a first-person perspective, it is not a character in the sense of a figure with a backstory who engages with events in the story world through a distinct voice. The "character" in *The Witness* is, according to the shadow cast I cast on the ground, recognizably human. I am able to interact with the physical elements of the islands, but it is simply that there are no obvious markers of story beyond my engagement with the puzzles and my observations of the world. As Blow puts it: "Thematically we wanted you to be completely alone" (No Clip, 2017), and this sense of isolation is evident in the use of the distant first-person perspective, the lack of other in-game interactions with characters, "radio play" moments in which the story was revealed, and the sparse sound design, which is overwhelmingly silent.

However, just because there is silence, it does not mean storytelling techniques are not at work, for even though Blow may identify himself as a designer, rather than a creative writer, *The Witness* employs a huge number of techniques commonly associated with narrative media, such as pacing, atmosphere, mystery, and point of view. Relatively early in the game I enter an orchard of pink blossoming trees. The puzzle squares in this section are branching, and it takes me a few moments to realize that their solutions can be found by observing the branches of the trees surrounding me (Figure 7.3).

This moment forces me to tilt my perspective in order to locate apples in the trees and to follow the lines of the tree branches that are echoed in the puzzle squares. In this way, it is not simply that the puzzles act as rolling tutorials, but that the landscapes themselves start to feature as prompts for how to shift perspective and look closer at the physical world in the game. In the words of Blow himself: "the panels in The Witness are a 'substrate for communication' (between the designer and the player) (2016)." Indeed, these puzzles provide a

FIGURE 7.3
The Witness

Shifting perspectives.

glimpse at how the environment of the island becomes an increasingly important aspect of the game, in which the story elements of the game are conveyed
more through interacting with visual cues in the game world than through
engaging with a narrative design based on linear story development.

However, as I move through the game, I also stumble upon other more
familiar narrative hints or devices that are placed within the game world.
At the site of a rusting shipwreck, I find a small rectangular item, like a
thumb drive, on the floor of what must have been the ship's bridge. I click
on the item, and an audio log begins: "A ship owner was about to set to sea
an emigrant-ship. He knew that she was old, and not well built…" The clip
goes on to tell a story of the shipowner's doubts about the safety of the vessel,
but his decision to trust in faith and providence. The ship piles with emigrant
families and sets sail, only to sink soon after. The narrator of the story reflects:

> What shall we say of him? Surely this, that he was verily guilty of the death
> of those families … He had acquired his belief not by honestly earning it
> in patient investigation, but by stifling his doubts. And although in the
> end he may have felt so sure about it that he could not think otherwise,
> yet inasmuch as he had knowingly and willingly worked himself into
> that frame of mind, he must be held responsible for it.

(William K. Clifford, 1874)

At first, I imagine these audio logs may deliver a kind of backstory narrative of the world. I google William K. Clifford and find he was a mathematician and philosopher. Wikipedia lets me know that he developed a type of "geometric algebra" to map geometric objects and that he was against "blind faith" in that he argued for evidence as the ethical basis for belief. While these details are interesting, I don't initially see any connection between the Shipwreck story and the game world—I assume the clip must be important because there are so few moments of text in the game—so I continue playing. As I move through other parts of the landscape, I am particularly taken by the other human figures I find among the ruins: they appear to be statues, or bodies preserved by lava or stone. I find these static, silent figures with their arms raised in prayer, or despair, or gathered in a group as if seeking some connection with one another. In the absence of an overt character or story arc, I begin imagining story possibilities of my own—that the island is an experiment gone wrong, that it is a version of Pompeii, and that the figures were part of a survivalist cult. Perhaps these are the survivors of the Shipwreck story, in a kind of purgatory? The openness of the story world in *The Witness* encourages these story possibilities (from the obvious to the more abstract), and the overall narrative design reveals an interest in ambiguity rather than linearity and plot.

This focus on alternatives to linear story and traditional character development is not a surprise. As Blow argued in his presentation *Fundamental Conflicts in Contemporary Game Design* (2008), "story games are inherently conflicted" due to an ongoing tension between story and play in traditional Triple-A design. For Blow, Triple-A games with stories commonly have "static stories" rather than "dynamic story techniques," games that focus on constant progression rather than challenge, and use prebaked delivery of stories through dialogue and cutscenes rather than exploring interactivity (2008). In many ways, the approach to story world in *The Witness* echoes Blow's earlier claims. The game explicitly situates challenge *as* the means of progression—puzzles unlock other puzzles, the environments provide clues to the puzzles, puzzles unlock various environments and, eventually, the environment itself exists as a series of puzzles. The emphasis shifts away from what Blow describes as the "story stuff," as the audio logs with story clues are very few—around six in the entire game—and also hidden within the world to such an extent as to be very difficult to locate (Giant Bomb, 2016).

As with *Horizon Zero Dawn*, I spend a great deal of my playing time of *The Witness* simply wandering or trying to get lost. Similarly, my exploration is fundamentally enhanced by the esthetic qualities of the game, not only the look but also the sound and feel of the game. But whereas *Horizon* uses environmental storytelling in relatively similar ways throughout, *The Witness* is continually challenging me to shift perspectives and learn new elements of play within the game world. As Jespur Juul has noted: "It seems the more time we invest in overcoming a challenge … the bigger the sense of loss we experience when failing, and the bigger the sense of triumph we feel when succeeding" (2013: 13–14). Failure, frustration, and repetition are therefore important parts of *The Witness*, aspects which certainly recall my experiences playing *Myst* many years ago.[4] Further, as I continue playing, I do find more pieces of disconnected text, in the form of audio logs or footage hidden throughout the island featuring philosophers, theorists, and artists reflecting upon notions of truth and belief—or ways of seeing. But it is not until the ultimate shift of the game occurs for me after roughly 25 hours of play that I start to connect these seemingly disparate elements of the game together.

I am in a wood with autumnal trees. Actually, I'm returning to solve a puzzle I had given up on a while back, the final puzzle of the series of squares in the wood. It's time to give it another shot. I am not sure how many puzzles I have solved so far, but I am confident in my ability to solve the squares, learn all the rules, and progress through the game. As I am crossing a bridge, I notice what looks like a puzzle in the side of the bridge. When I adjust my perspective, it becomes clearer. There is a single line that traces the sides of the bridge and emerges into the water. When I follow the line, I complete my first environmental puzzle![5] In a field close by, I now find curling lines of flowers that can be unlocked. It so happens that I was so focused on the squares as the chief mechanic that I had neglected to observe dozens of puzzles emerging in the surrounding landscape. I was like the shipowner who had refused to doubt the surface of things (Figure 7.4).

In this way, *The Witness* uses the squares both as the mainstay of the game progression and as a kind of huge red herring in suggesting from the opening moments of the game that they are the prime focus. Once the magnitude of the environmental puzzles are revealed—there are apparently around 130 to solve—the game shifts in focus in a profound way. As a player, I am exhilarated by these possibilities and begin to see the entire island as a series of codes and subtle nonlinear story moments. This is not narrative in the sense of a dramatic plot, but an understanding that the environment itself

---

[4] See Anthropy's comments on failure as a fantastic driver of narrative and gameplay in Chapter 6.

[5] In some ways, my lack of engagement with fan fora, reddits, or walkthroughs probably shows my age…who plays for 25 h only then to find a key mechanic!

FIGURE 7.4
The Witness

Environmental puzzles open narrative possibilities.

brings together several of the previously disconnected story elements—the audio clips and footage, the staring statue figures, even the title of the game itself—so that they enter into, I would argue, a kind of dialogue. This dialogic exchange is the central feature in the game's approach to story elements and takes place between the player, game designer, game world, gameplay and the story hints, and story secrets. Gamefeel in *The Witness* leads to storyfeel. This is not a dialogue in the traditional narrative sense but more about interconnecting relationships and ideas: that truth and perspective are shifting and mutable and that it is far too easy to get caught up in a limited, even dogmatic, viewpoint. Circularity is a key thematic too as, fittingly, near the "end" of the game I return to where I started, the long dark corridor in the ruins of the fortress.

Conclusion

In contrasting storytelling techniques from the Triple-A title *Horizon Zero Dawn* with *The Witness*, I have been interested in how creative writers for games are expanding narrative techniques, ludic immersion, and environmental storytelling to enhance the experience of games. Rather than concentrating on the linear narrative of *Horizon*, I concentrated on how my experience of playing was deepened through my engagement with the nonlinear and nonverbal aspects of narrative design. I suggested that, rather than linear narratives, Triple-A games have the potential to show how contemporary game experiences of story can be increasingly meditative, meandering, and innovative in the ways they blend game progression with story development. Turning to *The Witness*, I explored how in the detailed environments of open-world games puzzles can be both tasks and tutorials, and also moments that can connect the player's experience to the world, both built and imagined, in the game. And, just as this connection has the effect of enhancing gamefeel, so does gamefeel have the potential to enhance the experience of the story world. Specifically, I contend that one of the fundamental challenges for creative writers of games is to allow space for new storytelling techniques and interactions that are as much about the accumulation of story experiences than they are about linear narrative arcs.

However, just as a character or story arc typically develops through the course of a linear narrative, it is also important for nonnarrative storytelling techniques to continue to expand and change throughout a game. For *Horizon Zero Dawn*, the multiple narrative devices laid out in the prologue section of the game are fruitfully linked to the initial building of the story world and the development of the character. Yet, as the game grows in scope and scale, the environmental storytelling techniques remain largely static. In terms of deepening the *storyfeel*, my later experiences of Vantage points are similar to the first three—they do not change with Aloy, and beyond the rising difficulty of the combat (which is negated by skill, strength, and weapon upgrades), the wider game begins to rely heavily on the narrative flow and Aloy's own growth as a character. The scope of the linear narrative increases in depth and scale, yet there seems a lost opportunity to develop other aspects of storytelling. Indeed, while *Horizon* gives an idea of how video games are expanding the definitions of storytelling, it also suggests that Triple-A studios might further reflect on how writers can also enhance the environmental design of games. Several of these aspects are evident in *The Witness*, a game "without a story," yet which employs sophisticated storytelling devices that challenge our understandings of not only what stories can do in games but also how they might feel.

While completing this chapter, I return to *Horizon Zero Dawn*. I am still only 58 hours in, and I doubt I'll ever complete the entire game. There are simply too many aspects of the world to explore. With two children under 2, I can barely dress myself (let alone them), but I wanted to return and see if

I could move a little further through the main campaign. As I arrive back in the game, after a 6-month absence because of needing to play other games for this book, I am rusty. But while I can't train an arrow as fluently as before, it's surprisingly easy to set off again through the world. Aloy is still good company, and I consider that someday I might even make it to the *Frozen Wilds* DLC. I notice the ambient sound design and pause for a moment to take in the nighttime sky. It might seem incongruous to write about games that I may never finish, but this is my experience of playing at the moment. There is time to start games but never enough time to finish them. Instead, what I am looking for are moments like I have described in this chapter, moments when the feeling of playing is so embedded into the world that the story—even if that story is as illusive as during *The Witness*—seems to arise from the world, rather than exist as a parallel experience, a distraction, or a frustration. Not only that, storytelling (be that linear, fragmented, or environmental) also helps to enhance and shape the world of play. Or, at least, my experience is that it does. Perhaps it's not that epic games aren't made for me, but more that I need to play them differently now or I need to emphasize a different approach to time and play and narrative.[6] And this makes storytelling for games so exciting at the moment that the stories in games not only *are* different but also seem to have barely scratched the surface of the potential for new avenues of play and new avenues of experience.

Gamefeel leads directly to storyfeel, and exploring storyfeel is where the narrative designer or creative writer can advance contemporary game design.

---

[6]Anna Anthropy highlights an interest in different approaches to time and scale in Chapter 6.

8

Interview with Damon Reece

Based in Adelaide, Australia, Damon Reece is a narrative designer who specializes in open-world and modular narratives and has over 5 years' experience in the games industry. Damon has worked on multiple projects in a number of different roles, from writer to designer to social media marketer, and at the time of this interview was preparing for the release of Route 59 Games upcoming *NecroBarista*, a 3D visual novel released in August of 2019.

Damon gives a perspective on games writing that promotes social interaction and a wide range of player expression. In this interview, we discuss story possibilities in the shared world of *Sea of Thieves*, world-building in *Metroid Prime*, and modular storytelling in the indie scene. In a look at *NecroBarista*, Damon explains the many and varied jobs of a modern narrative designer, from producing a script to editing footage for a trailer, and laments a lack of consistency in the industry's approach to defining its roles and terms. We ask about the gap in innovation between the independent and Triple-A spaces, and the challenges of developing new storytelling techniques on a bigger scale. Damon points to the ever-increasing give and take between small and large studios but ultimately believes that a ground-up approach—educating writers in the technical aspects of game design—will prove most beneficial to the industry as a whole.

Timothy Williams: Damon, you've got a particular interest in open-world games and modular narratives. What are some recent examples of games you've played that have given you an interesting or unique story experience?

Damon Reece: The past few days I've been playing through *Destiny 2* with my partner. She has played through all of it already, but this is my first time with it. I've gone through the base game over the past few days and just started the first expansion pack last night. Before that, I was really enjoying *Forza Horizon 4*. One of the things I've played most this year is *Sea of Thieves*, which is a really interesting example of a game that is fairly empty of the sort of content that players expect a game like it to have, and yet it somehow manages to make and follow through on the promise that players will have interesting interactions with other players. I'm gonna go into some context here. People around my age, and I'm 23, have grown up with games like *Half Life 2, Team Fortress, Garry's Mod.* When you're playing with other players, you are in these curated community centers. Everyone is hosting their own servers, some with mods, some without; some have particular vibes and rule sets. These spaces then become less of a competitive space and more of a social space mediated through the game. The *Sea of Thieves* game space just looks like an open-world RPG, but, for me at least, it is definitely not an open-world RPG in the traditional sense. I use that space to hang out with my friends and enjoy the space that I am in. If I run across another player, I don't know what is going to happen because everyone is doing something different. Some players are going around trying to sink other ships, some are having a good time pillaging and plundering from other players, and some players are doing more of a peaceful play style, collecting animals and enjoying the environment. Shortly after the release, they added a megaphone item, which lets you project your voice chat further at the cost of not being able to hold a weapon. Sometimes, I'll roll up on an island and I'll hear, echoing over the waves, "hey, we're friendly, don't shoot us!" I think that's wonderful because then I'll hop on the horn with, "yay, we're not going to hurt you either; we'll park on the side of the island out of cannon range." Then you can go over, and they might pull out an instrument and start playing, at which point you're hanging out with another player in an entirely nonstructured encounter. The game has pieced you two together to have a good time, and you organically decided to have a good time together. *Sea of Thieves* achieves the best emergent storytelling I've ever seen.

EP: That sounds great! I had no idea that the game was having that sort of effect.

DR: It helps that the game is ridiculously stunning. It is a gorgeous game and a well-designed space to hang out in.

WC: Would you say, Damon, that part of what makes *Sea of Thieves* successful in that way is precisely that emptiness that players might not have expected?

DR: I don't know. I would say they need more content. Without the framing of "anything could happen," I don't think it would be as successful as it is. It is a very unique case in modern games. In games like *Dark Souls*, for example, players run into other players, and a specific sort of interaction will always take place that you'll have prepare for, whereas in *Sea of Thieves*, the content in the game *is* the player interaction. So many games have tried that and utterly failed to pull it off, but this one has done okay.

TW: That's a really interesting way of looking at how a social narrative can play out. As a narrative designer, you must enjoy exploring these different ways of producing and curating story. I'm interested in the distinction between a "narrative designer" and a more conventional "games writer." How would you define these kinds of roles?

DR: I think there is a distinction, but I also think there shouldn't be. A writer writes. Traditionally, in your classic *Gears of War*-type game, the game designers and level designers have all the content unlocked, and writers pad it out with dialogue and barks and maybe write some cutscenes.[1] Those writers are not really having an influence on the game or content design. A narrative designer, particularly in the indie space, has a lot more control over what is happening in a holistic sense. As a narrative designer, I really like to be talking to as many people on the team as possible. I want to figure out what is going on, how can I help out, how I can make this content better. I'm talking to producers, asking, "what are our budgets? What

---

[1] A "bark" is a short clip of character audio, such as NPC chatter, that gives the player context-specific information.

can we do with the amount of time and money that we have to make the game as cool as possible?" On any given day, I can be writing stuff, but I can also be designing a game system or whipping up mock-ups of UI [user interface]. I'm making sure everyone is on the same page in regards to how we'll be conveying the narrative. With *NecroBarista*, I just finished the scripts, so now I move onto a social media role. I spent most of yesterday setting up a really fancy marketing calendar in Google Sheets. As a narrative designer, I touch everything on a project because even something like marketing is narrative. I'm conveying a narrative to people who might be interested in buying our game. If I'm making a trailer, I'm specifically editing together footage to convey a narrative that evokes a particular feeling in a potential player. I would much rather have less traditional writers in games and more narrative designers. That's because the more that we have closely interlinked game design, content, and narrative, the better. If you just bring in a writer and say, "hey, put a story on this game," nine times out of ten that story is going to suck.

EP: Yes, I think that's a common theme in a lot of the interviews we've done. We very much agree. That exchange and interchange of ideas across disciplines is so important. How does that work for something like *NecroBarista*? How are you feeling about that process, and what are some of the interesting moments that have come out of that?

DR: I'm going to sound like a massive hypocrite because I've been sitting here saying that games aren't movies. But *NecroBarista* is an entirely linear game that is written almost exactly like a stage play.

TW: I think it markets itself as a visual novel with a very cinematic style. So I think that is okay as long as it knows what it is, which it does.

DR: Yeah, and also I think there is definitely a space for traditional writing skills, particularly in visual novels. Visual novels largely play it safe with game design and narrative trickery. A visual novel is probably the best space for a traditional writer to start out in games.

EP: When Tim and I were playing the demo for *NecroBarista* at PAX, we both noted that text and language was part of the texture of how you move through the game. There were nods to a hypertext past, and we were wondering if some of those things were already part of the design process when you came into the picture, or was that interest in language something that you brought to the project?

DR: I've been on the team at Route 59 for about a year; I joined shortly after Games Week in 2017. I've recently been going through all the old demos of the game for some promotional stuff and, interestingly, it used to be intensely hypertextual. Everything had paragraphs and paragraphs of text attached to it. Unfortunately, I think in a game like *NecroBarista*, all that text took away from the main narrative thread. In the current build, we've got those object-inspection sequences between scenes. The player is placed in first person, walking around and inspecting stuff, and I think that works better. I've been following the project since it was announced in 2015, and the thing that got me really fascinated was that they had an intense hypertextuality that added a real depth to everything. That interest for me comes from *Metroid Prime* and the ability for Samus to equip different visors on her helmet. One is a combat visor, one is an x-ray visor, and one is a scan visor. The scan visor pops up with these little notes around the environment, which players can then scan to get a little bit of flavor text about the environment. It's a mechanic that is ripped from the inspect function in a point-and-click game, but in *Metroid Prime*, it adds so much to the atmosphere and the environment. The story is about returning to a place, and something has begun to corrupt it and is bringing out its darker side. If players inspect a bit of moss, it will say, "this moss has changed recently due to radiation exposure; it's DNA shows clear signs of being different now." That's fantastic, especially because it's a game on GameCube, so you can't have super resolution textures or close up detailed models. That is such a smart way of adding depth and flavor to an environment.

TW: Yeah, it seems almost like a kind of nodal storytelling. You've got experience with these different storytelling models. Can you talk more about some of those distinctions—modular narrative, systematic narrative, etc.?

DR: The industry is fantastically inconsistent with what it calls things. I wouldn't necessarily call the scan nodes in *Metroid Prime* a particular kind of storytelling, because it is still a linear game; you're still progressing from point A to B with very little choice in how you approach stuff. In regard to modular storytelling—modular is the idea that you have, as a very basic example, a big map of an ocean, and there are a bunch of islands in the ocean-

TW: This is just *Sea of Thieves*, right?

DR: *Sea of Thieves* would be great for this actually. In this example, if players go to an island and do a quest, they will make a particular set of decisions with a couple of different factions or personalities involved. Then they can go to any other island and the choices they made on that initial island—including what they've picked up, who they've made happy or angry on that island—those choices will carry over to any of the other islands in this world. This is because the narrative system is built in such a way that it doesn't care in which order you approach it. It takes into account what players have done previously, even if what they've done previously is nothing. You could reshuffle these islands, you could put in different islands and remove some others, and you're building these specifically to respond to player choice in a really interesting way. Games like *Sunless Sea* and *Sunless Skies* by Failbetter Games, or *Voyager* by Bruno Diaz, are all really simple and nice examples of modular storytelling. Systemic storytelling is the idea that you have a bunch of game systems that are designed to interact with each other. *Caves of Qud* does this fantastically well, as does *Dwarf Fortress*. In *Caves of Qud*, players are in this surreal post-post-postapocalyptic world populated by animal factions. So you might have the Rude Coyotes and the Backstabbing Rabbits—I'm not sure if these factions are actually in the game, but they serve as an example. When players encounter one of these creatures, they can choose to trade with them or share water. If one of these factions has a bad relationship with another faction—say the rabbits don't like the coyotes—if you help the coyotes, the rabbits will have a lower opinion of you because you have interacted positively with their enemy. This also means that the player doesn't have to be an ingredient in these interactions. Players can walk onto a new screen, and in the example the developers have given for this, there might be two creatures from opposing factions who spawn next to each other and have just started annihilating each other. Players could go through a series of actions to try and repair the relationship between these two factions, permanently changing how the world reacts and changing that social web between nonplayer characters (NPCs).

TW: That's interesting. I think it kind of plays into something Anna Anthropy discusses. She talks about the perfect video game being a clean, unmuddied mechanical idea that translates perfectly into a storytelling idea. This also points to that intersection between mechanical design and narrative design. Would you say that's what this sort of systemic storytelling is trying to tap into?

DR: Absolutely. There is this ideal of the perfect open-world video game where the archetypical gamer can kill whoever they want and do whatever they want. I want that game, but for very different reasons. I want the perfect mechanical simulation where there are more verbs than just "kill."

TW: I like that idea. I think we all want that. Going back to what you said about the industry as a whole and its lack of a shared, uniform vocabulary—do you think we could benefit from some consistency across the board?

DR: I think so, yes. Particularly in the indie world—it's a scene that thrives off sharing information, and there is tremendous value in sharing information. GDC[2] makes loads of money every year through getting people to pay for information that should honestly be free. I have a particular dislike for communities where information or resources that could be shared freely are withheld. I do think codification is worth it, and I would love to see more consistent sharing and understanding of information and techniques. Sharing information doesn't make you weaker; it makes everyone stronger.

TW: That leads into something else I wanted to ask about, and that's this idea of the continued democratization of game

---

[2] GDC is the Game Developers Conference, an annual meeting of developers from all over the world.

development. You're a proponent of programs like Yarn and Ink, and you were a designer on Jacquard too.[3] Anna Anthropy talks a lot about Twine and Bitsy. How do you think this increased accessibility of games development tools is changing the industry?

DR: I think it's great because nowadays the main barrier isn't in tool kits and information; it's in resources. It is hard to get into game development if you don't have the resources of hardware or connections. It is even harder to get into commercial development unless you have a lot of money behind you. What Film Victoria does with their game development grants is fantastic. I would love to see more of that. The democratization of making games doesn't lie in the availability of tools. While I'm going to keep doing my best to share those tools, I think that is mostly a solved problem, and it is a problem that is going to keep solving itself because Unity and Epic Games have clearly seen the benefits of sharing their tools and tool kits. The main barrier now is people having the time and the education. Here in Australia, educating people on how to make games is definitely not a solved problem.

EP: How do writers fit into that? Do you think of them, ideally, as being trained not only in narrative design but in more traditional game design as well?

DR: Absolutely. I studied briefly at a local game development school, and everyone in the room was a programmer. If you're going to go and learn how to make games you should not be taught specifically how to use one tool set. Those are useful skills, but the more important stuff is the concepts. When you're writing, or narratively designing a game, the most applicable skill set is a working knowledge of theater. Video games are not movies or books, but they are essentially a very, very complex theater.

EP: What do you mean by that? Are you talking about the production process; the idea of working with a team with different visions—a story team, a design team, and so on? Or are you talking more about the audience?

---

[3] Jacquard is a narrative design tool built to utilize the Yarn scripting language.

DR: It's definitely both. It frustrates me a lot when a writer has been moderately successful in another field and comes into games expecting to do well without having studied on their own beforehand. Mediums like interactive theater are so different to screenplay writing. In games, you're giving players choices, but you have to be so careful to present choices that they're actually going to care about and actually going to want to choose.

WC: And do these sorts of ideas and lessons apply right across the spectrum of games, from the indie scene up to Triple-A? Can you speak a little bit more to the creative give and take between those different spaces? Could there be more of that happening between them?

DR: The Triple-A space is about 5 or 6 years behind the indie scene at any given point, perhaps further, depending on how innovative your storytelling techniques are. I don't know if indie development necessarily has anything to learn from Triple-A, because the scale of what is happening there is so irrelevant to indie development. I'm less interested to see what happens in Triple-A and more interested in the tier below that—studios like Arkane, who made *Dishonored* and *Prey*. Even though those games are obviously very lush and pretty, they're not gigantic productions from a studio of hundreds and hundreds of people, and that means they have a bit more space to innovate. Any storytelling innovation that's particularly potent is going to trickle up to the big studios from indie stuff eventually. Something like *Tacoma* by Fullbright is a good example. It's one of the best examples of how video games are like immersive theater; it's worth dropping everything and playing it right now. As a sophomore project following *Gone Home*, it pushes the idea of exploring a space and delivering narrative through that to a whole new level, and I would kill to see more stuff like it in bigger, more expensive games.

TW: Hopefully, it's just a matter of time. Let's talk about another game you worked on—*Hacknet: Labyrinths*. I spent a brief amount of time with *Hacknet*, and I found it incredibly difficult. How does challenge—and, in my case, player stupidity—factor into your writing?

DR: That's an interesting one. It's not something I've thought a lot about personally because Matt Trobbiani, the lead designer of *Hacknet*, ended up doing most of the design work. In *Hacknet: Labyrinths*, there is a chat room that players are constantly connected to, and if he'd had more time, I would have recommend having a hint system that slowly drip-feeds information straight to the player as they take longer and longer to solve something. The chat room is a really vital part of that expansion; having the live chat and the characters bouncing off each other, it could have been a really potent tool for communicating hints and tips to the player.

EP: It's good to get these insights into how you think as a designer, with that real focus on the play experience, as well as a writer. How do you see those roles developing in the coming years? What are some of the futures of narratives in games? Do you think new technology might present new ideas for you, or are there other types of narratives that you're really fascinated to explore?

DR: I am really excited to see bigger games using modular design, because I think it is a fantastic way of building content. In terms of technology, I'm not good at speculating on what is going to be exciting. However, VR is another great example of why game design is like writing for theater—you're literally building a set and populating it with props and actors. I don't know if games are going to change that much in the near future, but, that said, I'm very excited to be proven wrong.

9

Dear Reader
Virtual Reality and the
Narrative Frontier

Why would a video game begin with a book?

We're at Eddie's house, playing with the PSVR, PlayStation's recent foray into the world of Virtual Reality (VR). Will is wearing the headset, and Tim and Eddie watch on in amusement as he swings his head about in equal parts wonder and uncertainty. He's in an ancient library—high windows filter shafts of light that reveal specks of dust floating down from above. On a lectern is an ornate manuscript, the kind of old-fashioned book we associate with fairy tales and goblins. The title is written in a rune-like font: *Moss*. Will tests the controller, swinging open the first page to the rich sound of parchment crackle. Doing this requires mimicking the action of picking up a real page, and it's strange to watch him interact so earnestly with something that isn't really there. The pages appear yellow with age and are blank at first, but then a map appears. It resembles something out of *The Lord of the Rings*, and the effect is familiar and comfortable. Another turn of the page and the title emerges amid a woodland scene—grasses and flowers in the foreground and the trunks of large trees backlit in the distance. And then a voice, cool and female, as if from out of the book itself: "Your time has come at last, Dear Reader." So, we are readers of a story. And players, too? This is the new realm of VR, one that promises exciting possibilities for both storytelling and immersion in a game world.

In this final chapter, we explore two recent examples of storytelling for games that, while in different technological formats, reveal a similar preoccupation with how creative writing for games can enhance the world-building possibilities for the medium. We begin with an analysis of Polyarc's *Moss* (2018), exploring the ways in which VR allows for new elements of perspective within a narrative to deepen the connection between in-game characters, environments, and the play experience. We follow this with an examination of another puzzle-adventure story, *The Gardens Between* (2018), from independent outfit The Voxel Agents, to suggest how a seemingly minimal game without any dialogue or text, or the technology of VR, can nonetheless reveal how narrative design for video games is growing in ambition and scope. Indeed, while it is customary to link technological advancements with formal innovation, the future for storytelling in games has as much to do with embedding creative writing techniques alongside those new technologies, as it does with promising new kinds of experiences of play.

Moss

The opening address to the "Dear Reader" turns out to be more than just a nod to the nostalgia of an old-fashioned authorial voice. As Will continues through the old tome, the voice begins to tell a story. "They called it the Cinder Night…" This narration reinforces both Will's dual position as a reader and a player, as well as the familiar storybook tone of the world into which he is about to plunge. The game contains two main characters, both controlled to some extent by the player, and this is a big part of how *Moss* begins to unveil its story. First, there is Quill, an intrepid mouse adventurer, who starts the game wandering in the lush undergrowth of a forest. She is controlled in the traditional ways of a third-person platformer—walking, running, and jumping—and this familiarity helps to ease Will into the gameplay experience. Quill soon discovers a glowing blue orb with magical properties, known as the "Glass," and this development alters the nature of Will's interaction with the game. He now begins to interact with the world not only as Quill but also as a second character, the Reader, a spectral entity that hovers over every scene and who can aid Quill in negotiating her surroundings. "She was not exactly sure what she roused, but she felt no danger from the being silently peering down at her." The Reader occupies the camera point-of-view, using God-like powers to control various aspects of the environment—holding open doors, moving platforms or plinths, causing hostile creatures to become immobile. It is the interrelationship between the tiny figure of Quill, who moves through the levels and interacts with

FIGURE 9.1
Moss Bookcover

Dear Reader… (©Polyarc Inc. With permission)

---

the world from within, and the Reader, who watches over and influences the world as if externally, that is the core gameplay and central world-building device of the game (Figure 9.1).

Quill's uncle, Argus, has been kidnapped, and her homeland has been overtaken by a fire-breathing snake. Quill sets out to save Argus and restore peace to the world of Moss, guided along the way by a sparkling fairie creature, a Starthing, and the Reader. The action moves back and forth between the narrated story, as "read" in the library, and Quill's playable sequences, in which she and the Reader must solve environmental puzzles and fight enemies to progress. The Starthing describes this as being "Twofold," hinting both at its thematic and literal significance in the game world. Twofold not only refers to the synergistic relationship between Quill and the Reader but also suggests a new way of experiencing story in VR, in which the player's sensory perception—the interplay between their physical body and the VR headset, headphones, and controller—lends them to believe they are "immersed" in the game environment.

Through the development of more accessible technologies, VR is finally emerging from science fiction into the realm of the everyday. PlayStation VR competes in the gaming space with Oculus Rift and the HTC Vive, and while the cost of these headsets remains prohibitive for many players, narrative designers are beginning to more fully explore the storytelling possibilities of the medium (Morgan, 2016). But it is still early days—most VR games do as much reveal to the limitations and challenges of working with the technology as to suggest its possible future. Early successes have tended to reflect particular genres, such as flight simulators, in which the player's stationary position is aligned within the context of the game world.

As a result, a reliance on shock and awe, particularly in horror games, has been the primary storytelling ingredient in VR games to date.

Indeed, before playing *Moss*, we each took turns with a variety of the PSVR's most celebrated titles, intrigued by the promise of something genuinely new. And yet, the technology's major selling point—that the play experience feels more real and more visceral than in traditional games—is also perhaps, at least as far as storytelling is concerned, its greatest frustration. The most common feature of VR games remains a promotion of immersion above all else, resulting in the reduction of narrative possibilities down very specific genre lines, in which the player's fixed position—a cockpit, a car seat, an office chair—provides the opportunity to observe but not to fully interact. The result is that VR games, rather than suggesting new ways to *include* the player, are in fact employing traditional narrative devices, such as cutscenes, to keep the player at bay.

But that is not the case with *Moss*. Indeed, while Polyarc's debut explicitly draws on the classic beginning, middle, and end structure of a linear narrative, it does so as a means to explore, with a range of methods, the storytelling potentials of the new medium. One such method is evident midway through the game, as Quill boards a raft and makes her way along a river, soon coming aground on a beach. Tim is wearing the headset now, and he tracks the scene with a craning neck as Quill is suddenly surrounded by high cliffs, stretching sands, and vast, still waters, and the outline of a castle in the distance. We return to the library, where the story emerges from the book once again. Tim flips the pages, and the narrator tells of how it is on that beach that Quill finally meets the Starthing, a "strange, winged creature" named Aderyn. They converse by the side of a campfire, learning about each other's plight, until Quill, exhausted from her journey so far, falls asleep. Aderyn stands, emerging from the page of the book, directly addressing the player/Reader/Tim:

> Hey, ghostface. A lot of folks have been waiting for a Reader like you to return. I know I have. I'm going to scout the castle up ahead. Keep her safe, ok?

We mention this scene for two reasons. The first is Aderyn's literal emergence from the book in speaking directly to the player. This narrative technique, used often in traditional games, is heightened in *Moss* where the VR world encourages a more intimate link between character and audience. The dialogue suggests that their twofold interaction with Quill is vital to the game and story progression. The rules of the story world allow for what feels like a direct social interaction—Tim is being hailed by the game. As Brooke Maggs

FIGURE 9.2
Quill and the Reader

Embedding player and character within the storyworld. (©Polyarc Inc. With permission)

has written, social interactions like this, taking place within a game, confirm "the player's presence in the story world and provide information about their role and identity" (2016: 6). As such, that notion of "twofold" suggests a literalization of the immersive effects that VR can enable, as the perspective of the player is embedded in the physical world of the story (Figure 9.2).

Video games have, for many years, employed dual complementary playable protagonists as a gameplay and narrative technique. The idea of two characters with different skills and attributes, whose cooperation is essential to progression, has obvious attractions for design. Indeed, many of the industry's biggest recent successes have utilized such a formula: *Brothers: A Tale of Two Sons* (2013), *The Last of Us* (2013), and even *God of War* (2018). However, in *Moss*, the player's God-like perspective embeds the character of the Reader in the dynamic progression of the story, generating within the player a sense of responsibility through social presence. As Maggs suggests "a narrative technique unique to VR is to have characters recognise and respond to the audience [the player] creating a sense of being socially immersed… of being present (as a social being) in the narrative" (2018: 6). In *Moss*, the player/Reader is both the audience of the story and an active participant in shaping it, simultaneously controlling Quill and existing outside the game. This creates a level of uncertainty around defining the player's role, which is another example of how many of the ideas and questions of traditional gaming experiences can be more deeply explored in VR. As Greg Costikyan has pointed out, uncertainty is one of the primary reasons we play any kind of game—whether video, board, live action, or tabletop (2013). He suggests that there are many types of uncertainty operating in any one video game; in our view, part of the reason *Moss* excels is because three of these types—solvers uncertainty [manifested in the challenge of solving the game's puzzles], player uncertainty, and narrative uncertainty—all run parallel, and are all heightened by the immersive nature of the tech.

The second reason for focusing on the beach scene is that it allows for the player to pause and regroup, both in the game and in the real world. Just as Quill finds herself yawning by the campfire, so too is the player—who at this point, if playing the game in one sitting, has been wearing the headset for an hour and a half—forced to slow down. The narration here is unhurried, the moment in the library providing an opportunity for reflection and even relaxation. Indeed, Tim chose this very moment to remove the headset and take a break. Such moments are extremely important because they highlight how narrative design for games must also respond to the current capacities of the technology as interacting with the player's body in real life. Marathon gaming sessions, familiar to many in the traditional sphere, are simply not possible in VR—the headsets are fairly heavy, our eyes become fatigued more quickly, and it is not uncommon to feel somewhat nauseated after long periods of play. Storytelling for early VR games, then, must take each of these factors into account, and, ideally, use this knowledge to speak to a game's narrative progression.

Following on from Aderyn's direct address to the player, we return to the beach as our little mouse friend wakes up to find herself alone. A hidden passage is revealed, and it transports Quill back to the woods. The story is moving to its conclusion, and, not unlike *The Last of Us*, this final act presents an exhausted protagonist unsure of whether she can continue and prevail against overwhelming odds. However, whereas Naughty Dog's game merely exploits the player's growing emotional bond with its characters, in *Moss*, it is the character herself who actively underscores that bond. Quill literally turns to the Reader/player and asks for support. At this low point in the narrative, just when she needs us most, Quill is able to call upon the player. The Narrator states:

> She felt a gentle touch of warmth and mustered the strength to look up. The Reader was still there, expressionless as always, but unwavering in their loyalty.

In this way, Quill is referring to the symbiotic or twofold relationship that has developed between her and the player/Reader. And it comes as a surprise, for while previously she seemed to interact with us in minor ways— a high five or a happy squeal—such moments were primarily examples of contextless gameplay. The effectiveness of this particular scene instead relies fundamentally on three strands of the game's design working in tandem. The first is immersion; the VR technology gives the illusion of the player being embedded in the scene—a virtual body in a virtual world. The second is that the construction of gameplay, which emphasizes that the world of *Moss* is one in which the Reader as a character works in unison with Quill, is built into the narrative. And the third is a combination of the first two; the game's VR mechanics—our means of interacting with the game world—supplement its potential for immersion and the development of its characters in the context of the story itself.

Our experience playing *Moss* is not purely one of heightened immersion. It isn't that VR is the ultimate "empathy machine" (Milk, 2015), but that the shifting perspectives allowed in VR gameplay, and the ways in which the overall experience might be explored alongside new types of storytelling, are an exciting narrative frontier. The position of the player as both inside and outside the game world—in the words of FromSoftware's Hidetaka Miyazaki, "this sense of existence, but at the same time this sense of nonexistence"— sees a complex relationship between player, character, and the virtual world (Tach, 2018). In *Moss*, we occupy multiple roles—reader, God-like figure, controller of Quill—and our physical bodies become a bigger part of the experience, too. Interactivity is no longer mediated in the same way—the design of a typical video game controller has remained largely unchanged for the past 25 years—and VR headsets allow for 360° movement, which can open up new dimensions of a level, exponentially increasing the possibilities for new gameplay systems. Additionally, VR has seen the rebirth of such hardware peripherals as Sony's Move motion controllers, relics of a past generation, which can dramatically enhance the interactive experience. By actually altering the physical process of playing games, virtual reality has the potential to reshape how game stories are both conceived and enjoyed. And yet the future of storytelling in games should not necessarily rely on the advances of technology; sometimes, it's just as useful to look to the past, to traditional storytelling practices that are available to everyone, when embracing interactivity in creating meaning.

The Gardens Between

Released in September 2018, *The Gardens Between* is a deceptively simple puzzle adventure that follows two friends, Arina and Frendt. It is an independent game, made by The Voxel Agents, with minimalist level design and no dialogue

FIGURE 9.3
TGB Home

A narrative without text. (©The Voxel Agents. With permission)

whatsoever. The story, which explores how we interact with our childhood memories, is told entirely through visuals and gameplay. At the menu screen, we are presented with an image of two small houses on a gray city street. It's raining—the houses are overshadowed by looming apartment blocks and powerlines. A train rushes by in the background, up on a raised track. Each house has a single lit open window, bright in the gloom, which together illuminates the path between them. At the end of this path, in the very center of the frame, is the silhouette of a treehouse. The story starts here (Figure 9.3).

Pushing "Start" on the menu screen takes the camera forward, down along the path, as the sound of the rain swells with the musical score. Another train goes past, as two figures become visible in the treehouse. Frendt pulls a cord, and a naked globe illuminates the rough interior of the space, and of Arina, who sits across from him. There is a crash of thunder and lightning, and suddenly everything slows down, and then the scene starts to flow backward. There, between the two figures, appears a glowing orb, a ball of light. There is a kind of pulse, and then a flash, and the background fades away. For a brief moment, the treehouse seems to float in time, before descending into a black screen.

It's a bit like *The Wizard of Oz*—Arina and Frendt, spinning through space. They land on an island, a tiny island, and it's clear—we're not in

Kansas anymore. Arina and Frendt slowly get to their feet. The broken remains of the treehouse lie behind them. The island comprises mainly a great big pile of boulders, stacked haphazardly, and a number of seemingly random possessions, which seemed to have slipped through the time gap along with the children themselves. There's a cardboard box labeled "Bath Room" sitting on a red trolley, and a cricket ball, and a toy airplane, and the items hint at the narrative background of this game world. This is childhood, and nostalgia, explored not with prose or dialogue, but imagery—there is an immediate sense of the personal in every one of these physical objects, and a clear through-line from creative conception to development. The Voxel Agents are small studio based in Melbourne; their members grew up in the 1980s and 1990s. Anna Anthropy reflects in our interview in Chapter 6 on how interesting it can be as a player to get a sense of the author behind a game, and these objects undoubtedly carry a clear voice throughout *The Gardens Between*. It's almost melancholic, as if Frendt and Arina are unpacking (or packing away) their shared childhood memories.

The opening level also reveals the game's primary mechanic—a time shift that enables the player to run time forward and backward by toggling the left stick on the controller. This system most obviously recalls the time-shift mechanic in Jonathan Blow's *Braid*, and in fact the island setting might also suggest his more recent work. However, unlike in *The Witness*, the islands here each represent a different level of the game; in order to progress, the friends must navigate a path to an endpoint, which takes the form on each island of a rock altar that enables a jump through time and space to the next stage. The camera tracks around each island, following the characters and allowing the player to observe not only the specific path ahead but also each level as a whole, including any hints into environmental puzzles that need to be solved by manipulating time, and, by association, the objects, within the them.

The Gardens Between plays with our ideas of childhood nostalgia, in a similar vein to *Moss*. But whereas Polyarc crafts a fairytale world to draw on the familiarity of shared illusion, The Voxel Agents instead finds magic in the mundane, exploring the disparate remnants of childhood. Each island is a kind of memory bubble, and the reward for solving it puzzles a brief flashback to the scene from which those memories were born. The first of these sees Arina on the front steps of her house, playing with the toy airplane. Next to her lie a stack of cardboard boxes on the red trolley. Frendt approaches and waves, and the scene ends. It's a form of cutscene—player interaction is practically nonexistent—and yet intriguingly subtle. There is no dialogue, no linear narrative progression—it's just a glimpse into these

FIGURE 9.4
TGB Couch

Memories as a catalyst for gameplay. (©The Voxel Agents. With permission)

characters' lives. These memories generate meaning most powerfully in how they link explicitly to game progression. They represent of kind of mirroring between the island worlds of the strange, timeless present, and the elusiveness of the past, combining to evoke in the player the very sense of nostalgia that lies at the heart of the game's story.

It is on a metaphorical level that *The Gardens Between* develops its narrative most fully. As Arina and Frendt continue on their journey, navigating the messy contents of a rumpus room—an old couch and a bowl of popcorn, and a makeshift cubby house—each image takes on a more dynamic presence, a presence within both the playable levels themselves and the succeeding flashbacks (Figure 9.4).

One of the advantages of a textless game is that the player is invited more openly to project his or her own sensations onto the play experience. Each island requires for Frendt and Arina to navigate a glowing orb, and we came to think of these orbs during our playthrough as little moments of déjà vu. That idea of cycles, of actions performed and undone, is reinforced profoundly in two consecutive levels. The first presents an environmental puzzle involving a Mario-esque platformer on a television screen. A black bird needs to be hit by a purple beetle. The second level shows a bowl of popcorn overturned by a falling cushion. In the following flashback, Frendt and Arina are sprawled across the couch, playing that same platformer. Arina takes a piece of popcorn from the bowl beside her and throws it at Frendt's head. Time pauses briefly and then runs backward, and when the scene plays again, the television begins to jiggle, emitting a high-pitched noise. The black bird emerges from out of the TV, scuttling behind the couch. Arina releases the popcorn again, but the scene appears to be caught in a loop—the popcorn hits Frendt and time flows back once more. It's an odd moment, unexplained in any traditional sense, and instead invites interpretations that speak metaphorically to the game's themes. Most vividly, it suggests that memories and their associated nostalgia are perhaps not as fixed as they might seem. In this way, cutscenes in *The Gardens Between* feel less like static nonplayable sequences, and more like dynamic, moveable extensions of each individual stage. In combination, they seem to generate narrative possibilities.[1] The flashbacks remain integral to the play experience because of how harmoniously they reflect the themes of the story.

In a later level, about two-thirds of the way through the game—*The Gardens Between* takes about 2 hours on a first playthrough—Arina loses her jacket down a storm drain. There it is, hanging from a pipe, way out of reach. It soon becomes clear that, in order to progress, Arina has no choice but to lose her jacket forever. In many ways, this image represents the message of the game as a whole—we must lose things we love in order to grow. In fact, the time-shifting mechanic itself speaks to that theme, too. Frendt and Arina want to relive their friendship, but no matter what, no matter how far back they try to go, it remains a fact of life—and of video games too—that time must always move forward. In this sense, *The Gardens Between*, with such a deft consonance of form and content, is a perfect example of ludonarrative harmony (Figure 9.5).[2]

In the game's final moments, the fragile aspects of memory start to take on a physical form, as the islands themselves are pulled up into the sky. Arina and Frendt follow a path upward, but this is a dark moment—the storm from the very beginning has come back. Lightning flashes, a fog descends. We pass the television, but the screen is smashed, and other objects seem to be spiraling away into space. As the island begins to violently rotate, the player feels the game itself apparently escape control, but not for long. Arina and Frendt are together and safe—the path has cleared before them but destroyed the things they love.

It may be a much smaller game than many of the others we've covered, but *The Gardens Between* is no less notable for the way it negotiates storytelling

---

[1] See our interview with Brooke Maggs in Chapter 2 for a discussion of the writer's role in creating these narrative possibilities.

[2] A clear counterpoint to Clint Hocking's observations on *Bioshock* and other titles like it.

FIGURE 9.5
TGB Frustration

Ludonarrative harmony. (©The Voxel Agents. With permission)

in an interactive medium. It manages to generate character, empathy, and story meaning without any dialogue and without diminishing the complexity of its gameplay systems. Puzzle games are nothing new, but The Voxel Agents have built a game world in which the puzzles themselves are a major thematic element of story, and vice versa. Perhaps this is a new branch of Neil Druckmann's "language" of narrative games.

Conclusion

In this chapter, we've explored ideas of storytelling and immersion in the VR and non-VR game worlds of *Moss* and *The Gardens Between*. These two recent examples bring an awareness of how creative writing can enhance games in a way that also deepens our engagement with the world-building possibilities for the medium. They reveal how narrative design for video games is growing in ambition and scope—from the integration of changing visual perception in *Moss* to the deceptively simple visual storytelling of *The Gardens Between*. Despite their significant differences in development, both games reveal how the harmonic alignment of play and story confirms the importance of closely engaging with writers in the design process. The results speak for themselves.

10

Interview with Lincoln Davis, Tam Armstrong, and Shauna Sperry

Lincoln, Tam, and Shauna are part of the team behind Polyarc's 2018 PSVR game, *Moss*. Polyarc was founded in 2015 with the aim to build innovative games through collaboration. Located in Seattle, the studio currently comprises 16 members, spanning artists, designers, animators, writers, and engineers. Lincoln is the head of publishing and communications, Tam is a lead designer with a background in game systems and artificial intelligence, and Shauna works both as a writer and in HR.

As *Moss* is Polyarc's first game, we took the opportunity to ask about the challenges of bringing a new team together to create a story-driven experience for virtual reality (VR). We discuss the importance of inspiration and ambition, looking outside the video game space, as well as how design iteration can be the key to problem solving in the development process. The team also considers how modern technologies can breathe new life into traditional storytelling techniques and imagines the ways this relationship could develop in the future. Additionally, Lincoln, Tam, and Shauna provide specific insights into how the varied skill sets of creative teams work in tandem to produce a coherent story in a highly complex technological space. The discussion explores both the similarities and differences of working with VR when compared to more traditional video game experiences, highlighted in a reflection of position of the player as both inside and outside the game world. The team hints at how this unique perspective might influence VR storytelling in years to come.

Eddie Paterson: I suppose the best place to start when talking to a group of game designers is with your tastes as players. What are the types of games you all enjoy playing? And how did these games potentially influence the early thinking of *Moss*? Or do you play games that are completely different to the types of games you create?

Tam Armstrong: I'm an omnivore of games in general. I don't rule out any particular genres or types, and that includes analog games like card games and board games. The video games that I've played the most recently—*Breath of the Wild* is the big recent one that I've put quite a lot of time into, but that was after *Moss* was finished. While we were working on Moss, I was playing *Bloodborne* and a little bit of *Counter Strike*. I think those games are so different to *Moss*, and that was probably part of the reason I was playing them. It was a distinct break because I just needed to reset for a different kind of content when I went home.

Shauna Sperry: I grew up with an Intellivision, computer games, and later a Super Nintendo, and am a big fan of those old school games—*Donkey Kong Country* for SNES being my all-time favorite. I don't play many games these days, but writing is a passion of mine and Polyarc gave me the opportunity of a lifetime to help with the story and writing for *Moss*, even though I am not necessarily an avid gamer.

Lincoln Davis: I enjoy several styles of games, but I tend to gravitate toward platformers and sports games on the console the most. However, I've played more and more mobile games since having kids. I have three kids—nine, seven, and five—so my games have been centered around games I play with them or within the 15–30 min of free time I'm able to squeeze in a day. That said, since working at Polyarc, we've definitely dabbled in a lot of VR. And, of course, *Fortnite*.

EP: It's interesting to hear about your backgrounds in gaming and how games today fit into your lives and work. There are similarities there but also clear differences. How did that affect the design process on *Moss*? Were the narrative and game design progressing hand in hand, or were there other orders to the process?

TA: Our studio has decided that we are gameplay first, and then the characters and story are very important supporting elements. I think we sit somewhere in the middle in contrast to companies that are entirely focused on mechanics, or alternatively, to companies that really want to deliver on pure narrative without a lot of interaction. We try to balance the two, with design leading. The practical example of that in *Moss* is that the thematic elements of the small animals and the world that they live in were by-products of us trying to design to VR's strengths. Early on, we were looking at VR, and we were concerned about how we would do locomotion, and while we were confident someone was going to solve that well, we were not sure we wanted to spend energy there when there were plenty of other places to spend energy. Following the decision to avoid locomotion, we decided that if players were not going to move around the world too much, we needed to make accessible gameplay that was more or less within arm's reach. We also knew we wanted to have a protagonist in the game as a character other than the player, although we did want room for the player as their own character in the game as well. The lack of locomotion together with a reachable gameplay space meant to us that we needed a tiny character. We thought about how we were going to theme the game with these constraints, and that was when the tiny animals came to the front of the pack. There were several options, after some sketches drawn by our art director, of all these little characters—we thought of toys, aliens, making the player giant, among others. At that time, there was no story, but once that spark was set by the theme, the story began to follow quickly. We outlined a broad concept of what the story would look like for this tiny character we had. She was named something completely different at the time—she was a grumpy little old man named Remy. We started building the game and iterating on the storyline alongside the mechanics, as we wanted the story to support the game and the game mechanics, while also contributing emotional impact in its own right. I think, philosophically, that's the way we would approach game design in the future as well—make sure we nail down the core principles of the gameplay, and then the story is really built on that in a mutually supportive way.

TW: I love the idea that each aspect of the process can intersect like that. It seems very collaborative. I think I read somewhere that Quill's fluency in sign language actually came out of an audience reaction online to a tweet of an animation test?

TA: Quill signing was one of those mutually supportive things where an idea that seems good for the game design becomes integral to the story—by collaborating on how to rationalize it and how to build it into the game. That particular inspiration came about because our animator, Richard Lico, made a test animation of Quill using sign language. The response was so overwhelmingly wonderful that we couldn't see ourselves not putting it in the game. When people reacted the way they did, we thought it was a wonderful opportunity to integrate this into the character's backstory and into the theme of the world, which led to a richer character design with more nuance. We already had animations of Quill making generic gestures in her cheeky attempts to communicate to the player what they were doing wrong in the puzzles, but signing gave us more room for her to communicate.

WC: That particular mechanic is especially effective in VR, where the character can directly address the player in such an intimate way. But what were some of the challenges of working with that technology, especially from a storytelling perspective? And how did you overcome them?

TA: We usually try to think about them like they're constraints. Every medium has a set of constraints, and in contrast to other visual mediums, like film or television, the freedom of shot selection and camera angles is a constraint that the form of VR storytelling presents as a challenge. We tried to take inspiration from other mediums that may have similar constraints. For us, we were trying to think about the construction of the rooms in which the story was occurring as stages in a stage play. We were thinking about using light and sound and movement to guide the player's attention and thinking about writing scenes that could work inside of those settings without the need for rapid transitions through many environments.

EP: One of the things we noted about our experience of playing
     Moss—that was different to our experiences with other VR
     games—was the framing of the narrative. The storytelling
     esthetic of the book, and the fairy-tale world that players
     are stepping into, was something we all really loved. How
     did some of those ideas develop? Were they in place from
     the beginning or did they emerge later in the process?

TA: We had the idea that it should be a fairy-tale world from
     the beginning, but the storybook concept grew in signifi-
     cance over the course of development. Both Shauna and I,
     as lovers of books in general, have similar positive feelings
     that you just expressed—the comforting idea of storytell-
     ing in that form. In the very beginning, the idea was that
     the moments in the book were going to be end caps for
     the game, as homage to the animated Disney film *Sleeping
     Beauty.* We love that opening the book is the player's input,
     an expression of saying, "alright, I'm going to play now."
     It started there and that's all it was for a while, but then as
     we were trying to provide more motivation for Quill and
     the player to care about proactively proceeding through the
     game, we decided we needed more moments to deliver nar-
     rative beats. We realized, for the size of the studio and the
     scope of the project, it was not possible for us to tell all
     of the narrative beats through in-game animation. We had
     to come up with another way to do get the story across,
     so this book concept that started out as end-capping the
     game prototype became another option. We asked our-
     selves, "What if players go back the library? What if the
     story cross-fades between the book and the gameplay more
     frequently?" Suddenly, the book was more important than
     just a marker, and it became a part of the world. Once the
     players were spending more time in the library, more than
     just as a main menu, that motivated us to start adding to
     the layers of mythology, and it all started growing together.

EP: Yes, and I think the other effect for us as players was having
     that little break from the gameplay, where particularly in the
     VR experience, there is a level of fatigue when you are start-
     ing out. Having that slightly calm and passive period was
     really helpful to us for finding our way through the game.

TA: That's wonderful to hear. We like those moments of pacing, and we care a lot about the comfort of our players; hence, early decisions like the lack of a free-moving camera. Not that every game we create will follow the same set of constraints, but that was a very high priority for *Moss*—to make it as approachable as possible for the widest possible audience. There is a deliberate attempt to spread the storybook moments out in a certain way and to design the pacing of the gameplay to fit that. It's one of the ways *Moss* gives you permission to stop playing for a moment or even to rest if you're going to keep playing.

TW: The notion of accessibility is interesting. You mentioned *Sleeping Beauty*, and *Moss* does indeed borrow from that fairy-tale esthetic and mythology. But, like a lot of fairy tales, it also hints at some darker themes. How do you tow that line between being accessible to everyone—*Moss* could be enjoyed by 6- and 60-year-olds alike—while still writing something mature and meaningful?

TA: In our earliest discussions around forming the studio, we decided we wanted to spend our time working on things we felt regenerated by. There are other kinds of games you can make with more explicit content and violence, many of which are wonderful games by the way, but we were having a hard time imagining working on them day in and day out over the course of a couple of years. That's a cultural decision for the studio, and it says nothing about any other studio that makes different decisions, but that was important to us, and so that set a tone of finding ways to make our games compelling by other means. We wanted one of the keywords to describe our games to be "joy," and that opened up our design philosophy to everybody. Given the relatively small market for VR today, we wanted to think about how to make it appealing for *everyone*. It's our belief that kids generally don't get enough credit for their emotional capacity, although there are definitely some examples where the credit is given—the wonderfully layered films made by Pixar, in particular. We thought this layering of meaning was a wonderful aspiration for us to have as well. It's a way of achieving a breadth of feeling that could reach a wider audience. We tried to make sure we wrote genuinely that we weren't pandering. We looked at things like *Harry Potter*, a series that means something to people of all different ages and backgrounds. We tried to consider as wide a variety of perspectives as we could, because we were working to make sure there was something compelling for all of them.

EP: That also suggests that you were thinking about the story and the game together on multiple levels. A lot of VR experiences frequently rely on an element of shock or surprise, an adrenaline rush at a certain moment, and one of the things that we felt about *Moss* was that the medium was being used in a more multilayered and considered way. Shauna, I was hoping you might reflect on your process within the story team, and how you used and enhanced some of the elements that are particular to VR in ways that perhaps other teams haven't thought about?

SS: The VR platform provided us with this amazing opportunity for both physical and emotional interaction. VR actually transports you there as a character in the story. You're present in the world with Quill, so it's this truly unique storytelling experience where the action is being directed *to you*. Other mediums can break the fourth wall, but it isn't necessarily making you a participant. In *Moss*, you're part of the action and the interactions in the world, and we believe that the biggest impact from a storytelling perspective in VR comes from those opportunities for emotional interaction. At the beginning of the game Quill, right off the bat, is acknowledging the player's existence with surprise and intrigue. The two of you go through gameplay together, and you're responsible for healing her when she is hurt, or when she is asking directly for your help, and you know you've got to have her back in order to succeed; it really feels like she is relying on you as a true partner. These moments are all part of this emotional interaction, and these parts of the story result in an amazing emotional experience for our players. And, because of how VR complemented our storytelling, we were able to find success writing a story about partnership. There's actually this relationship arc between the player and Quill that is pretty cool. Granted, we didn't necessarily know we were doing any of that at the outset, but we were paying attention to the storytelling elements and implications throughout development in this new medium. We cared about it and iterated as we went.

EP: It's a fantastic notion, the idea of a relationship arc rather than simply a character arc. So you're saying that the realization that this arc was happening took place a little later in the design process? In the sense that maybe you started with a character arc—Remy's arc, as it was—and then this notion that the player relationship was kind of deepening came in later. Is that right?

SS: I think our awareness of it changed throughout development, especially as we continued to iterate on the writing. Players start off meeting Quill for the first time, and you're just acquaintances who are learning that you can do fun stuff and work together to solve problems. Over time, you're doing this in more complex ways, and you start becoming attached to each other. You feel the depth of this partnership and the need for each other—both in terms of having complementary skill sets in gameplay and from a friendship, support perspective. We found that players deeply cared about Quill and were genuinely upset when she was upset, and they wanted to do anything possible to help her through that. Quill acknowledges that she needs you by her side to have any hope of getting through the great obstacles ahead. You're a true partnership. We became more aware of that connection as we got deeper and deeper into the writing process.

TA: I would add to that, to really support Shauna's point, the relationship between the player and Quill evolved pretty dramatically from the start. To give you an example—we had to remind ourselves when we were writing the story beats to include the player as a character. That was strangely difficult to write, because it was so easy to write about Quill and Argus and then forget that the player is supposed to be present in the scene. It was a deliberate effort that we got better at over time, in large part thanks to Shauna's rigorous adherence to the creative research that we were doing, and the principles behind the writing that we were doing. It evolved into a very important thing where if you had asked us what the themes of the story were when we first started, that bond with Quill wasn't one of the primary themes. It always mattered because we knew you were in the game with Quill, but the whole shape of the story began to bend itself around that theme of cooperation and partnership.

TW: One of the game's real strengths is its pacing—how that relationship is developed from beginning to end. Danny Bulla [a designer at Polyarc] has said that it's "the cadence between moments of sadness and excitement that give texture to *Moss's* narrative," and I think that ties into what you're saying here. Looking back at the game as a whole, how did you manage that cadence in the writing process?

SS: From a high-level storytelling perspective, I think everyone can agree that we *want* to feel different emotions while watching a movie or reading a book, so that you can have this meaningful, complete-feeling experience. But in the gaming world, where there are many differing opinions about what role story should even play, you can ask yourself, "how does having a spectrum of emotion *benefit* gameplay?" We believe the answer to this is that it raises the stakes. For example, if players have the gameplay task of having to defeat the serpent Sarffog, then that is going to mean more if Quill and the player have just had this intense near-death experience, an emotional moment of loss in the story. Quill has just hit rock bottom and is clearly struggling emotionally, but she also wants to avenge her friend Aderyn and save her Uncle Argus. The player wants to help, and to make Quill feel better, and therefore becomes more determined and invested than ever in gameplay tasks because of this emotion. We aimed for our narrative goals to complement gameplay goals and help create purpose and pressure to keep playing. If you look at the game as a whole, these emotions come out in different ways throughout, and every area of the game has a different feeling and vibe. We, as writers, hope it evokes different emotions along the way, leading to this overall feeling that you've had the complete, purpose-filled experience that most of us want with any story.

WC: One of the ways you achieved that, I think, is by managing a consistent balance between the many different roles of the player. You've said how important it was to recognize the player as a character. A real strength of VR is the opportunity it presents for toying with perspective; Quill is a third-person character that you're controlling fairly traditionally, but then there's this god-like figure that you *inhabit*, too. And on top of that you're also able to manipulate the environment, while Quill acknowledges your presence in the game. How does writing for VR work differently, in regard to managing perspective, from writing for other types of games?

TA: I can absolutely comment on how the writing process went from the *Moss* perspective, but I'll qualify that I don't have any way to contrast with writing for other games because I've never done that before. There were some interesting conversations—we had a set of conversations early on wondering if the player was going to feel any dissonance guiding Quill around the level while at the same time being their own character. We were worried about interacting with that character and interacting with the world as two separate roles, and how that might produce a strange sense of disconnection from Quill. The narrative design solution there was to make sure our animator, Rick, had the opportunity to provide moments of autonomy inside of the game for Quill to develop her character. She is able to remind players that she is her own person when it isn't going to impede the gameplay—or, ideally, when it is going to compliment the gameplay. Fortunately, complimentary is where we ended up most of the time. During storytelling moments, we had to also make clear that Quill has a certain personality and a point of view that you as the player don't necessarily share. A big part of realizing her was making sure to have a character profile for her and knowing who she was as a separate individual from the player. We hoped that having the clarity of that in the writing and her performances would support the feeling that they are distinct individuals. That is how we navigated that interesting perspective shift where you are sort of playing both characters, hopefully eventually making it clear that you're really the Reader, and Quill is there with you.

WC: Those moments of potential dissonance—I actually found that some of my favorite moments in the game where when they were teased out because I did become aware of a dissonance, but not in a negative sense. It heightened the sense of Quill being her own character. I think the way you can play with that dissonance, and have it evolve across the course of the game, is really interesting. I think you were definitely successful in that.

TA: We're very glad it was effective. One of the fun early moments in the prototyping process was when players would guide her, and they would make a mistake—they would walk her off of a ledge or get her killed by one of the enemies. They would start apologizing to her and telling her that they weren't going to let that happen again. Players were so readily projecting individuality onto her. We realized there was a very powerful connection there and that this capacity to connect to another character is actually a significant strength of the medium. You can do that in other mediums, but there is something about VR in particular where the capacity of empathy for characters is amplified.

EP: You mentioned earlier how those emotional connections were a huge part of your ambitions for *Moss* in the first place. It's clearly one of the game's biggest successes. I've got a couple of questions that come out of that. Looking forward, what do you see as some of the other possibilities for storytelling in VR? What techniques can you imagine building on in future projects? And Lincoln—what do your kids experience when they're playing with the technology? What are some of the things they point to as the most exciting, engaging moments?

LD: Well, first of all—audiences are conditioned to playing games or experiencing entertainment by sitting on the couch with the controller in their laps. At times, we feel like we have to give people trying VR for the first-time permission to move around to really experience the world. But when watching my kids or other kids at home or at trade shows, the amount of movement and emotion they feel naturally when experiencing VR is eye opening. You see them move around freely right from the get go; you don't have to encourage them to do so as you do with an adult because they're not conditioned to having the controller in their lap.

A special moment for me with my kids happened the first time each of them played *Moss*. See, every time a revision was sent around the office, I would bring it home and read it to them for a bedtime story. So when they were finally able to play the game, they already knew the characters, they already knew the story, and it became real to them. Quill wasn't just a video game character; she was a real mouse that I've been talking to them about for a long time. She was just sitting inside the PlayStation. They know she's not real, but knowing her story and interacting with her in her world… she's real to them.

EP: That's really lovely, and it points to something we're trying to emphasize in this book—we don't think you can write about game stories without also taking into account the physical interactions of play, and the idea of moving across a physical, real world as well as a virtual one. You need to consider all of it—the physical, the emotional, and the technological—in order to talk about storytelling potential.

TA: Absolutely. I think the agency that you feel in a game is one of the ways they engage you so strongly. In VR in particular, the physical performance that is possible—and I mean performance in the sense of performing an interaction, or pantomiming out a joke for your friends in multiplayer—these are very fundamental human activities. Having the ability to be physically expressive in games has a lot of incredible potential, because then everything players are experiencing lines up—the fantasy that is in your mind, the things that your eyes are seeing, and the feeling of your body moving through the space. Something as simple as petting Quill evokes emotions from a side of your mind that is harder to get to than if you're pressing the "pet" button, for example.

TW: That holistic perspective, a consideration of how every aspect of the design process can manifest in play—that kind of brings me back to something I was going to ask at the beginning. Tam, you've said of *Moss*, "you're reading it, but also writing it… it's kind of weird." What do you mean by that?

TA: Not the most articulate I've ever been.

TW: Perhaps you could rearticulate then?

TA: I was probably really excited about playing with the idea that you're immersed in a different reality in VR. You're a real person and you put on this headset, and you're transported to this other place. That is the same experience I have when reading books. I open the book and I'm not in my room anymore. It was an appealing notion for a book nerd to imagine that that we were playing with that concept in a very real way. The fantasy that you always have as you're reading a book, that the things that are transpiring are real—we could really add to that because we could actually give you agency to some extent over the events. That is where the lines of the reality begin to blur in our mythology. If you're reading about it in a book did it happen in the past, or is it happening now? The implications of that became the basis for the lore of the whole *Moss* world. Without overwhelming the player in this introductory story, we wanted it to be deep enough to tell a much bigger story. We started to set that up in this game, but we didn't want to alienate anybody by spending too much time emphasizing that part of it… But we did want that complexity for some freedom in the future. So we ended up in this place where the library is the magical dimension, or plane, or spiritual world, depending on the terms you want to use, and it has the reflection of the world of *Moss* contained within it inside of the books. That gave us the potential to have pretty heavy implications, which may go unsaid in the game itself, about what it means to read and write inside of those stories. I should add to this, kind of out of order— as a game developer, I've been cognizant of the fact that what we've built is a simulation. We had the opportunity to merge all three of those layers—what VR can do, what game development means to us, and what transporting into the fantasy of books means to us. It all came together in the context of *Moss*, and then lent itself toward that mythology that we wanted to start building. Once we had that book metaphor, we could have other metaphors, too—the narrative threads, the lives of the characters existing inside of the books. If you've heard that phrase, "everyone is the hero of their own story"—we imagined that is essentially what the books are. In the library, all of those stories being told are potentially from the point of view of the inhabitants of the world. I don't know—it can do to your brain what the Tesseract at the end of *Interstellar* does to your brain, and that's a fun feeling, so we hung onto it.

11

Interview with Tomasz Bednarz

Born and raised in Poland, Tomasz Bednarz is now director of Visualization at the Expanded Perception & Interaction Centre (EPICentre) at the University of New South Wales Art & Design, where he specializes in analytics and big data. The EPICentre is a research center that undertakes visualization research with groundbreaking technology in the fields of art, design, science, medicine, and engineering. Tomasz has worked in a range of areas, including human-computer interaction, simulations, computer graphics, and games.

In this discussion, Tomasz reflects on a childhood devoted to tinkering with computers, which has led to a career today spanning multiple disciplines and applications. He considers story as a part of his work, but not its essence, but can imagine the ways in which modern and future technologies might transform storytelling in the social realms of virtual (VR) and augmented reality (AR). Fundamentally, Tomasz believes in the power of technology to change the world for the better, recognizing the importance of grounding technological advancements in the human experience. In particular, he highlights the impact of his work outside the realm of video games, demonstrating the potential of combining gaming and film technologies to more broadly impact industry and culture in years to come.

Eddie Paterson: Your interest and expertise in video games and technology spans such a broad range. I noticed that you've got an old Atari in a cabinet in your office. Is that where it all started?

Tomasz Bednarz: It all started a very, very long time ago. The first computer I ever saw or played with was an Atari 130 XE, and the game *Donkey Kong*. My neighbors had the Atari computer, and I really loved the experience. I always wanted to have a computer. My parents went to the big hi-fi supermarket, and they got me a Commodore 64. I was very disappointed because everyone else had Atari, and suddenly I had Commodore 64. I didn't know that it had almost the same games, or maybe even better games. I plugged in the cartridge that came with the Commodore, and it was a football game. It was great! Then there were others—*Ghosts 'n Goblins*, and *Pacman*, of course. All those old-school games—that's how it started.

EP: So how did you get from there to where you are now, at EPICentre?

TB: It's a long story. Have you got 2 hours?

EP: Hmm, not quite. Maybe you could give us the highlights.

TB: Okay, I'll try to keep it short. I started with the games and the console—the Commodore. A couple of months passed, and I started looking at computers in a different way. I was interested in computer graphics, as well as how I could actually start programming the computer itself. The manual that came with the Commodore 64 taught users how to type the program and get the music playing. I would change a couple of hexadecimal values and get different instruments. I loved it—I could change just one number and have a completely different instrument playing. Those days no one was doing voice synthesizers, so for me it was like hearing a computer speak. That was a process, and I was superexcited about it.

In Poland, we had a Commodore 64 magazine, and there were hexadecimal numbers going through the pages—it was the machine code. You typed the numbers into the Commodore 64, and then you'd have a scroll, or some music, or some text, or silly graphics being displayed. I thought that was superfascinating, and so I started digging a bit more into programming.

Then the Omega 500 was released. We didn't have it at home, but I wanted a better computer. So I asked my parents, and instead of Omega, they bought me the IBM PC XT. What?! All my friends were playing beautiful games and playing music and so on, but I had this PC XT that was almost useless. It was the IBM box with OS file where you can copy files or open office and type text. I really hated that. But there were a couple of games I kept playing— *North and South* and *Civilisation*—the first one—and some others. I was really very curious about how this was done on PC. In the OS, you type the command code—you could display, let's say, the content of the file. But when you actually display the content of the file that's running the games, it's just a lot of junk on the screen. So I started looking at the assembly language. I thought that if I wanted to know how the computer works, then I needed to start at assembly. I started doing different experiments, and I decided actually to go to computer viruses, because it was superexciting. But I stopped after half a year to do something that wouldn't harm the community. I can tell you the story of when I went to the computer markets and gave out one virus on a floppy disc, and it spread across the globe. It was able to get past all the antivirus software packages. I won't give you the name—it's not important—but that's part of my history.

I was looking for something useful, so I decided to switch to computer graphics. I started actually connecting and writing programs that display pixels on the screen. And that was when I discovered something called the demoscene,[1] which is an underground computer art subculture. It's a very important part of a lot of today's games, because the best games and the best retail graphics were always demoed by demoscene artists. People who had early 8-bit computers and 16-bit computers were trying to use these computers to create the art in a way—running programs that track in real time, placing and synchronizing the background music. So that was one of the driving forces. Another was that we had these demoscene parties that were happening every couple of weeks. Pretty much everyone in Europe— France was very strong, Germany was very strong, Sweden, Finland, and so on. All the driving creative forces were

---

[1] The demoscene is an international computer art subculture that showcases small, self-contained demonstrations of computer programs.

based on limitation. We had competitions where the graphics had to fit on a floppy disc—that's 4 KB. You have to go beyond the limitations of your computer. You make lots of tricks in graphics and lots of tricks in mathematics, just to make sure they rotate the matrices very quick, throw the points very quickly, and put as many points on the screen as possible. And because of that all those people who were demoscene artists became very skilled at computer graphics, and lots of them—I would say maybe 50% of these people—are currently in the game development industry.

So I was doing that through high school, and then I went to University. I wanted to study computer science, but I took a look at the program and it was superboring. They were teaching things I already knew, so I decided to go and study something else that I thought I might find a bit more interesting. I went to study physics—I have masters in physics, which is awesome, because it's opened different areas that I'm very passionate about. Things like fluid flows, which link very closely with computer graphics. So I was always coming back to my roots. Lots of my exams and lots of special projects I was doing were around computer graphics and visualization. That's when I was actually shaping my skills and going into shortcuts, using my computer graphics skills to actually complete university. And after that, I got a PhD in Japan doing computational simulations of hydrodynamic flows, but my passion was always to come back into computer graphics. Visualization was a tool that was connecting everything—fluid flows, computer graphics and visualization, computational simulation sciences. I was trying to connect all of that together, and that's when I moved to Australia. I started working at James Cook University, a bit on visualization but also on computational fluid dynamics. I wanted to go back to computer graphics, so I applied for the job at CSIRO as a 3D visualization software engineer. We were doing projects with Rio Tinto— in a way we actually used gaming technologies to drive the advancement of the mining industry. You removed the operators from the very hot environment—Dunhurst in 45°—and put them in an air-conditioned room 3 km away. You put them in the front of big screens with the joy-sticks and all the sensory information coming through the screens. They can now operate as if they were there, except they've got a coffee machine next to them.

EP: It's a unique journey, Tomasz—you're coming from such a different perspective to the other people we've spoken to. We're much more familiar with story—most of our other interviews have been with writers or story-focused designers—but you've got this perspective on visualization and systems that is really fascinating. The visualizations you've shown me at the EPICentre—some of them don't really contain story. They're just information, or, as you say, they're a visualization of a pure mathematical equation or code. But then others *do* have a story attached to them. Do you play around with narrative and storytelling, or are you purely attracted to the experimentation within the code?

TB: Well, this may disappoint you, but I'm really not play-ing games at all these days. What I'm doing is translating whatever gaming technologies are currently on the market, and I can do this because I've developed games in the past. Basically, I connect the EPICentre—it's a bunch of differ-ent projects in many different directions. In a way, there's always a story. One of the projects we're actually starting now is in narrating—it's nodes that come from the very heavy simulations and telling the story of the processes, and how these simulations influence the outcomes of the simulations for the decision-makers. If you imagine a scenario—for instance, how to start the engine of a car—you can imagine 5,000 different ways that can play out, all about how you come from Point A to Point B. So you look at the physics of the engine, and so on, and then you can use computational simulation sciences to simulate those 5,000 different simulations at the same time, and that helps you make the best decision for the design process.

Coming back to the EPICentre itself—it's kind of a hybrid form of visualization. We're putting visualization analytics into different areas—art, science, and engineer-ing. We use the visualization asset, whether it's for telling a story or to deliver hybrid form visualizations, with the tools we have that allow us to access scientific discovery. One of our newest projects is treating PTSD. That's psychology and gaming technologies coming into the one place. It's done in a very twisted way—you can imagine the psychologist and patient sitting in the same space in the virtual world, and then when the patient is telling the story you start replaying the scenes. You're actually creating the scenes, so in a way it's like you're playing a game.

EP: So the patient would be telling the story of their trauma, and then you're recreating it as visualization for them?

TB: Yes. The whole idea of the trauma treatment—I'm no expert from the psychologist point of view, but I work with psychologists—they try to use the technology to advance the ways we look at trauma. The war veteran with experiences in the war is coming back, and they've got this PTSD that causes this big problem in their everyday life. What they do currently is set up 50 different sessions—it's done with pencil and paper with the doctor taking notes—and they go and repeat stuff until you trigger some memories and find the real source of your trauma. It's not visual—it's storytelling, in a way. You admit to some of the experiences you've had, and the trauma is supposed to go away. What we're trying to do is to use this technology to actually enhance the experience, to experiment with the vision and storytelling and sound, and possibly even smell 1 day too, so that when you're telling your story we can recreate it as you go. We're trying to actually recreate your memories, whether with very simple graphics or maybe something photorealistic, and then we can see what your biofeedback does. We can see how the memories really influence you.

EP: That really sounds like applying some of those lessons from a game design space into whole new areas. It's a combination of all sorts of methods. You mentioned biofeedback there, and its connection to storytelling. It suggests a future for not only how we might measure the way stories are affecting us, but it could also actually change, in a sense, how we write the story to begin with. We might find that certain stories affect us in certain ways. Maybe linear narratives are not as effective, in terms of biofeedback, as more fragmentary types of storytelling, or storytelling based in choices made by the player. How do you imagine new technologies like biofeedback entering into a gaming space? What are some of the adjustments that stories might have to make to accommodate that?

TB: Well, as far as biofeedback goes—I'm currently working with sensor networks to enable biofeedback processes of people when they're looking at the story. If you have arachnophobia, for example, we show a spider and we can perhaps detect a peak in the signal. So we begin with EPICentre and other platforms that allow us to measure that in real time. We measure things like heart rate and even your eye gaze—where you are looking at any given moment. And the story can develop depending on those reactions. So if you're building a horror story, say, then you're going to maximize the horror experience of the audience. You can find their weaknesses by measuring their biofeedback and then create the universe as they go through the story. So the simulations and the stories can go in many different ways.

TW: That sounds like an extremely complex form of systemic storytelling. How close are we to actually achieving something like that?

TB: That's part of the research we're doing at EPICentre—how far is it from the reality? I think all the bits and pieces are there. We have it up on all these platforms, so that's not a problem—it's just having the defined proper objectives of the project. I really believe that with storytelling through biofeedback, we can make stuff for a good cause.

EP: You mentioned earlier the idea of being driven by limitations. What are some of your biggest limitations at the moment, and what types of stories might still be able to exist within them?

TB: I'll start with technology. The UNSW has a couple of different visualization modalities, from traditional experience to VR and AR, and then going to the EPICylinder[2] and the hemispherical dome. These are all, let's say, immersive

---

[2] The EPICylinder is a 340°, 3-m tall data visualization environment, consisting of 56- to 60-inch screens that deliver an ultrahigh-resolution display.

environments, and each of these technologies has its own limitations. In EPICylinder, for example, you can see each other and which reality you're in. It's copresence in VR, seeing each other and experiencing the same VR, and being able to discuss face-to-face. But then what if you want to go into separate rooms? That's completely different, because you're wearing these wires that obstruct your field of view. So that's a limitation. As for the hemispherical domes—the current limitations there are that it's not interactive. So we've tried to change that—we've developed something called a high visualization system, which allows us to translate between different systems. So whether it's VR or AR or it's the hemispherical dome, we can translate most of the projects we have developed on EPICylinder into those other areas, and that changes everything. So by unlocking these limitations, we can explore different ways of looking at storytelling and data.

EP: So each of the different technologies can tell you something different? And then you're moving the stories across those technologies to experience them in different ways?

TB: Yes, that's correct. And there are different considerations within that. If you're sitting in the hemispherical dome, say, then the image will be different than if you were to render it on flat screen. You need to take that into account if you want to tell the story in a dutiful way. But it's fascinating—immersive technology allows you to do something, which wasn't possible. It can transport you to anywhere you want, it can allow you to become whoever you want to be.

EP: That's certainly the promise of immersive technologies as far as games go. We've played a lot of the more rudimentary VR systems—particular PlayStation VR. One of the things we've really found is that most VR gaming experiences rely very much on two elements—either a form of shock or a very linear narrative, or both. Most can be reduced to a narrative base from which something is narrated to the player and you move through a linear space. It's almost like a walking simulation. What we're interested in is where someone like you might bust those ideas of storytelling open. Where do you think the technology is heading, and how might different kinds of stories follow on from there?

TB: I have very some good colleagues from Pixar, and they actually construct lots of stories in a completely different way to how it was done before. As you know, creating linear stories, especially when you're doing animations, you create all these dot points that you have to follow to progress the story. The technology they are using has reached a point where not only you can have little computer graphics coming into immersive prototyping, but you can also do real-time ray tracing, where you can actually compose your story as you go. So if you don't like something, you can just come back and create different variations—you can change the textures and shaders, you can change whatever you can imagine.

EP: So you're getting a lot more control over the whole creative experience?

TB: Exactly. That's where the technology is going. They're developing at Unity a kind of gaming platform for movie creators, where you can change the graphics and expressions and everything as you go. And then you can replay it, reconfigure the scenes—it's supercool. At Pixar, they didn't use to have much procedural stuff going on inside the animations. But now, after the *Brave* movie, if you look at the trees, say, compared to a film like *Monsters Inc.*—they used to be static objects. These days, it's beautiful simulations everywhere. That's why the people are coming into place to make the computer graphics more realistic, and storytelling more realistic too, so it touches the emotions of the audience.

TW: It seems like there are so many ways that technology is changing how we tell stories?

TB: It's accelerating the process of making stories. Animation used to be very tedious work. Now you can do so much online, in real time, and that's where gaming technologies actually link in with movie graphics, visual effects, computer graphics, and ray tracing techniques. And things will keep changing in the next few years.

EP: Speaking of the future, at least as far as gaming is concerned—it seems that we're presented with two major options. One is a very technological future, where, as you say, the technology allows an acceleration of devices that might enhance storytelling in various ways. The other option would be a rejection of that future, on the grounds of accessibility, or a lack thereof. There's been a big movement in recent years toward more old-school development techniques—things like hypertext, for example. A lot of the independent designers we've spoken to are heavily engaged in that community and that sort of work. As someone who comes from a highly technologized background and workforce, can you see a link between these two futures? Can you foresee a space in which new technology is freely available and where narrative is played with as a key part of what that technology can do?

TB: When we talk about immersive technologies and immersive gaming, there is a still a huge gap in terms of accessibility. I went to a conference last Tuesday on VR and AR for manufacturing, and I was surprised—lots of people said they had never experienced VR in their life. It was actually quite shocking. It's the same if you look at the curriculum we have here. I ask students, "how many of you have played with VR in the past?," and more than half have never touched the technology. If I have to change the world, if I have to be a decision maker as to how it should be, I strongly believe the technology should be helping us to lead a better life. Imagine sitting with your friends, having beer, and one of them is telling you a story, and you can actually visualize the stuff he is thinking. Maybe you're using AR implants built into your eyes or your brain. That's where storytelling and technology is going. All the technological advancements will be augmented within us. And I think it's for good, because it makes people more engaged. Think about AI. I always say that AI requires lots of labor, but maybe in the future, we'll have robots doing stuff for us. Then we can focus on being friends with each other, writing books, and telling stories. I hope so.

12

Conclusion

We are lost in an orphanage. The children who live here know we exist, they want to play with us, so they leave clues and notes and instructions for us to find. If we complete tasks, helping the children in some way, we gain the ability to move back or forward through time and can travel to other parts of this story and see the effect of our actions. The orphanage is large and frequently creepy. We are a faerie, a sort of ghost; we are here and not here at the same time. So begins our experience playing FromSoftware's *Déraciné* (2018).

Video games are reimagining how we feel and experience stories. Not only that, they are altering the way we think about storytelling by creating vast worlds, intimate interactions, and playful encounters. In *Déraciné*, almost every limitation of the VR technology, from our tentative use of the motion controllers to the jagged animations and visual modeling helps to situate us as a strange presence in an unfamiliar story world. The experience of playing *Déraciné* frequently feels lonely, an intimate extension of the walking simulator in which our faerie presence might alter the story, but can never quite control it. As Walt Williams makes clear, "immersion comes from the dramatic experience," and it is the role of the creative writer or narrative designer to help refine and enhance this experience. In the introduction of this work, we described the multiple story possibilities and the epic scope of *Red Dead Redemption 2*, and here we end with the micronarratives of childhood fantasy and the idea that the fantastical worlds and creatures we dreamed up as children are emerging in new forms of storytelling. Once. Once upon a time.

This book has explored the possibilities for storytelling and world-building in video games by foregrounding our experiences as players and creative writers. Along the way, we've been lucky enough to draw on the insights of a wonderful group of writers, narrative designers, data visualizers, and theorists from the world of Triple-A to the vibrant dimensions of the independent scene. These experts have helped us to think deeply about what it means to be a creative writer in video games today and how writers are extending the boundaries of the medium.

We began this book with a discussion of what it means to be a writer in the games industry. Walt Williams shared his experience scripting blockbuster stories and explained why and how writers are essential to making Triple-A games that move beyond simplistic notions of combat and reward. Narrative designer Brooke Maggs echoed Walt's enthusiasm for innovative games storytelling and reflected on how writers for games can work within different production models to provide the architecture for rich story experiences.

In Chapter 3, Will led a compelling analysis of how *The Last of Us* extends the possibilities of linear video game stories, by paying attention to the unique "language" of the medium in ways that enable a curated player experience that is both interactive and emotionally engaging. Video game theorist Brendan Keogh provided a wonderful counterpoint to Will's conclusions, as he discussed the problematic elements of Triple-A narrative models and why true innovation may only be possible in the independent space.

In Chapter 5, Tim took on the *Metal Gear* series and explored the idea of the auteur in video game writing. He provided new insight into the legacy of Hideo Kojima in terms of narrative design and experimentation. In contrast, radical game designer and thinker Anna Anthopy encouraged us to move beyond cyclical discussions about open-world adventures and the promises of new technology, and instead to situate the possibilities of writing for games in the playful and accessible tools available online. Drawing on her own experiences as a designer, writer, teacher, advocate, and player, Anna argued that new developments in game writing are happening in the supportive and inclusive spaces of Bitsy and Twine.

Returning to the mainstream, Eddie turned to an examination of *Horizon Zero Dawn* and *The Witness*, to explore how narrative innovation and environmental storytelling can enhance gameplay and provide an experience of what we call storyfeel. Eddie's conclusion sits along our interview in Chapter 8 with Damon Reece who reflected on how online games have created new avenues for emergent storytelling.

In order to explore new dimensions for storytelling in recent games, Chapter 10 looked at two distinct examples of new storytelling practices in VR fairytale *Moss* and independent puzzle adventure *The Gardens Within*. Next, we talked to Polyarc Studio's narrative team about the challenges and possibilities of writing for VR, and whether the unique capacities of VR technology are changing the way stories in games can be conceptualized. In our final interview, we discussed future technologies with data visualization expert Tomasz Bednarz, including ideas of copresence in virtual space, bio-feedback in gaming and how advances in computing power may offer new points of view and increased interactivity in games.

This book is the result of a collaborative process. In emphasizing this, we moved between very subjective experiences of play to reflection from experts with the goal of revealing diverse trajectories of game experience, and a range of views on how creative writing is enhancing the storytelling and world-building capacities of games.

In *Once Upon a Pixel*, we have celebrated the role of games writers. But this is also a book for you. We imagine you as a video game fan, a player, part of a community, and, like us, someone who sees game worlds, and the stories within them, as a hugely exciting place to explore.

References

Aarseth, Espen J. 1997. *Cybertext: Perspectives on Ergodic Literature.* Baltimore, MD: JHU Press.

Anthropy, Anna. 2012. *Rise of the Videogame Zinesters: How Freaks, Normals, Amateurs, Artists, Dreamers, Dropouts, Queers, Housewives and People like You Are Taking Back an Art Form.* New York: Seven Stories Press.

Apperley, Tom. 2011. "Gaming rhythms: Play and counterplay from the situated to the global." Lulu.com. PDF e-book.

Bigl, Benjamin, and Sebastian Stoppe, eds. 2013. *Playing with Virtuality: Theories and Methods of Computer Game Studies.* Frankfurt: PL Academic Research.

Bissell, Tom. 2010. *Extra Lives: Why Video Games Matter.* New York: Vintage Books.

Bissell, Tom. 2013. "True-ish grit: On naughty dog's latest game, the last of us." *Grantland*, published June 12, 2013. Accessed June 16, 2018. http://grantland.com/features/tomcbissellcnaughtycdogclatestcgameclastcus

Blow, Jonathan. 2008. "Jonathan Blow speeches 'fundamental conflicts in contemporary game design,'" *YouTube video*, 104.55, published August 1, 2012. Accessed May 1, 2018. https://www.youtube.com/watch?v=mGTV8qLbBWE

Blow, Jonathan. 2016. "The witness." *YouTube video.* Accessed May 1, 2018. https://www.youtube.com/watch?v=UwBl7Rnkt78

Bode, Christoph, and Rainer Dietrich. 2013. *Future Narrative: Theory, Poetics and Media-Historical Moment.* Berlin: Walter de Gruyter.

Bogost, Ian. 2011. *How to Do Things with Videogames.* Minneapolis, MN: University of Minnesota Press.

Bogost, Ian. 2016. *Play Anything: The Pleasure of Limits, the Uses of Boredom, and the Secret of Games.* New York: Basic Books.

Cheng, Paul. 2007. "Waiting for something to happen: Narratives, interactivity and agency and the video game cut-scene." *DiGRA Digital Library.* http://www.digra.org/wp-content/uploads/digital-library/07311.24415.pdf

Conditt, Jessica. 2016. "Traveling through time with 'Braid' creator Jonathan Blow." *Engadget.* Accessed December 13, 2018. https://www.engadget.com/2016/01/21/traveling-through-time-with-braid-creator-jonathan-blow/

Conway, Steven. 2010. "A circular wall? Reformulating the fourth wall for videogames." *Journal of Gaming & Virtual Worlds* 2, 2: 145–155. doi: 10.1386/jgvw.2.2.145_1.

Costikyan, Greg. 2013. *Uncertainty in Games.* Cambridge, MA: MIT Press.

Delahunty-Light, Zoe (2017) 'Horizon Zero Dawn Review: "A world that begs you to explore every corner"' February 20, https://www.gamesradar.com/au/horizon-zero-dawn-review/

Dispain, Wendy. 2009. *Writing for Video Game Genres: From FPS to RPG.* London, UK: Taylor and Francis.

Druckmann, Neil. 2013. "GDA Toronto 2013 Keynote: Neil Druckmann, Creative Director & Writer, Naughty! Dog." *YouTube video*, 119.36, published October 2, 2013. Accessed February 9, 2018. https://www.youtube.com/watch?v=Le6qIz7MjSk

Dunne, Daniel. 2014. "Brechtian alienation in videogames." *Press Start* 1, 1: 79–99.

Flanagan, Mary. 2013 (2009). *Critical Play: Radical Game Design*. Cambridge, MA: MIT Press.

Franklin, Chris. 2013. "Errant signal – the last of us (spoilers)." *YouTube video*, 15.59, published July 21, 2013. Accessed July 11, 2018. https://www.youtube.com/watch?v=bAzqDgKYfiM&t=126s

Gallagher, Rob. 2012. "No sex please, we are finite state machines: On the melancholy sexlessness of the video game." *Games and Culture* 7, 6: 399–418. doi: 10.1177/1555412012466287.

Giant Bomb. 2016. "We play 'the witness' with Jonathan Blow." *YouTube video*, 1:40:45, published February 18, 2016. Accessed December 13, 2018. https://www.youtube.com/watch?v=jhEDARvLf90

Goldberg, Daniel, and Linus Larsson, eds. 2015. *The State of Play: Creators and Critics on Video Game Culture*. New York: Seven Stories Press.

Grounded: The Making of the Last of Us. 2013. Dir. Jason Bertrand, Matt Chandronait, Jeffrey Keith Negus, Ryan O'Donnell, and Cesar Quintero. *Amazon Instant Video*.

Hamilton, Kirk. 2013. "The last of us: The Kotaku review." *Kotaku*, published June 14, 2013. Accessed September 19, 2018. http://kotaku.com/theclastcofcusctheckotakucreviewc511292998

Herman, David. 2009. *Basic Elements of Narrative*. West Sussex, UK: Wiley-Blackwell.

Heussner, Tobias, Toiya Kristen Finley, and Jennifer Brandes Hepler, Ann Lemay. 2015. *The Game Narrative Toolbox*. Burlington, MA: Focal Press.

Hocking, Clint. 2007. "Ludonarrative dissonance in bioshock: The problem of what the game is about." *ClickNothing*, published October 7, 2007. Accessed March 3, 2015. https://clicknothing.typepad.com/click_nothing/2007/10/ludonarrative-d.html.

Jayemanne, Darshana. 2017. *Performativity in Art, Literature and Videogames*. Basingstoke, UK: Palgrave Mcmillan.

Jenkins, Henry. 2004. "Game Design as Narrative Architecture." *electronicbookreview.com*, published July 10, 2004. Accessed June 16, 2018. electronicbookreview.com/essay/game-design-as-narrative-architecture.

Juul, Jesper. 2011 (2005). *Half-real: Video Games between Real Rules and Fictional Worlds*. Cambridge, MA: MIT Press.

Juul, Jesper. 2013. *The Art of Failure: An Essay on the Pain of Playing Video Games*. Cambridge, MA: MIT Press.

Karabinus, Alisha. 2013. "What makes a game good, anyway? Narrative and gameplay in the last of us." *Samanthablackmon.net*, published July 23, 2013. Accessed May 9, 2018. http://www.samanthablackmon.net/notyourmamasgamer/?p=3101

Karabinus, Alisha. 2015. "Gaming narratives and the writer problem." *Samanthablackmon.net*, published April 4, 2015. Accessed May 9, 2018. http://www.samanthablackmon.net/notyourmamasgamer/?p=6660

Keogh, Brendan. 2014. "Across worlds and bodies: Criticism in the age of video games." *Journal of Games Criticism* 1, 1: 1–26.

Keogh, Brendan. 2018. *A Play of Bodies: How we Perceive Videogames*. Cambridge, MA: MIT Press.

Klevjer, Rune. 2002. "In defense of cutscenes." In *Proceedings CGDC Conference*, edited by Frans Mäyrä, 191–202. Tampere: Tampere University Press.

LeFebvre, Rob. 2013. "The last of us: Games as written." *Creativescreenwriting. com*, published August 6, 2013. Accessed January 24, 2019. https://creative screenwriting.com/the-last-of-us/

Maggs, Brooke. 2018. "Surveying VR storytelling: Investigating key terminology and the role of the procedural author." *TEXT* 49: 1–12. http://www.textjournal. com.au/speciss/issue49/Maggs.pdf

Milk, Chris. 2015. "How Virtual Reality Can Create the Ultimate Empathy Machine." *Ted Talk video*, 10:26, published March 10, 2015. Accessed November 11, 2018. https://www.ted.com/talks/chris_milk_how_virtual_ reality_can_create_the_ultimate_empathy_machine?language=en

Morgan, Rob. 2016. "Escaping the Holodeck: Storytelling and Convergence in VR/AR." *GDCVault*. Accessed September 13, 2018. www.gdcvault.com/ play/1023657/Escaping-the-Holodeck-Storytelling-and

Moriarty, Colin. 2013. "The last of us review: Survival of the fittest." *Ign. com*, published June 5, 2013. Accessed various dates. http://au.ign.com/ articles/2013/06/05/theclastcofcuscreview

Moss, Richard. 2017. "Roam free: A history of open world gaming." *Ars Technica*. Accessed December 13, 2018. https://arstechnica.com/gaming/2017/03/ youre-now-free-to-move-about-vice-city-a-history-of-open-world-gaming/

Mukherjee, Souvik. 2015. *Video Games and Storytelling: Reading Games and Playing Books*. New York: Palgrave Macmillan.

Murray, Janet Horowitz. 1997. *Hamlet on the Holodeck: The Future of Narrative in Cyberspace*. New York: Simon and Schuster.

Muscat, Alexander, William Goddard, Jonathan Duckworth, and Jussi Holopainen. 2016. "First-person walkers: Understanding the walker experience through four design themes." *Proceedings of the First International Joint Conference of DiGRA and FDG* 13, 1. http://www.digra.org/wp-content/uploads/digital-library/paper_318.pdf

Myles, Aaron. 2012. "Metal Gear Solid's Postmodern Legacy." *Nightmaremode. The Gamers Trust*. Accessed August 13, 2015. http://nightmaremode.thegam-erstrust.com/2012/01/04/metal-gear-solids-postmodern-legacy-part-1/

No Clip. 2017. "The Witness Documentary." *YouTube video*, 47:58, published April 2, 2017. Accessed May 1, 2018. http://www.youtube.com/ watch?v=YdSdvIRkkDY

No Clip. 2018. "John Gonzalez on writing horizon zero dawn – Extended interview." *YouTube video*, 43:15, published January 16, 2018. Accessed December 13, 2018. https://www.youtube.com/watch?v=a4P7uaaoRcM

Planells de la Maza, Antonio José. 2017. *Possible Worlds in Video Games: From Classic Narrative to Meaningful Actions*. Pittsburgh, PA: ETC Press.

Plante, Chris; Riendeau, Danielle. 2013. "Let's talk about: The ending of the last of us." *Polygon*, published July 24, 2013. Accessed various dates. http://www. polygon.com/2013/7/24/4548992/thecendingcofctheclastcofcus

Rogers, Tim. 2007. "Dreaming in an empty room." *Insert Credit*. Accessed October 17, 2015. http://archives.insertcredit.com/features/dreaming2/

Rose, Frank. 2009. "Metal Gear's Hideo Kojima talks conflict between games, stories." *Wired.com*, published March 26, 2009. Accessed February 18, 2019. https://www.wired.com/2009/03/of-the-worlds-t/

Skolnick, Evan. 2014. *Video Game Storytelling*. Berkeley, CA: Watson-Guptill Publications.

Smith, Harvey. 2000. "The future of game design: Moving beyond deus ex and other dated paradigms." *Witchboy. Witchboy.net.* Accessed December 13, 2018. http://www.witchboy.net/articles/the-future-of-game-design-moving-beyond-deus-ex-and-other-dated-paradigms/

Stanton, Rich. 2015. "Metal gear solid 2: The first postmodern video game." *Eurogamer.* Accessed November 9, 2015. https://www.eurogamer.net/articles/2015-08-16-metal-gear-solid-2-the-first-postmodern-video-game

Swink, Steve. 2009. *Game Feel.* Burlington, MA: Morgan Kaufmann.

Tach, Dave. 2018. "FromSoftware's Deracine is about a weird feeling that only exists in VR." *Polygon.com,* published June 22, 2018. Accessed June 27, 2018. https://www.polygon.com/e3/2018/6/18/17475530/fromsoftware-vr-deracine-e3-2018-hands-on-interview-miyazaki

Takolander, Maria. 2018. "What games writing teaches us about creative writing: A case study of The Fullbright Company's gone home." *TEXT* 49: 1–13. http://www.textjournal.com.au/speciss/issue49/Takolander.pdf

Upton, Brian. 2015. *The Aesthetic of Play.* Cambridge, MA: MIT Press.

Villamor, Mark. 2013. "The choice we don't know we make in the last of us." *Venturebeat.com,* published June 23, 2013. Accessed November 14, 2018. https://venturebeat.com/community/2013/06/23/the-choice-we-dont-know-we-make-in-the-last-of-us/

Wardup-Fruin, Noah and Pat Harrigan, eds. 2004. *First Person, New Media as Story, Performance and Game.* Cambridge, MA: MIT Press.

Weise, Matthew. 2003. "How videogames express ideas." *DiGRA Digital Library.* http://www.digra.org/wp-content/uploads/digital-library/05150.07598.pdf

Wijman, Tom(2019) "The Global Games Market Will Generate $152.1 Billion in 2019 as the U.S. Overtakes China as the Biggest Market," June 18, https://newzoo.com/insights/articles/the-global-games-market-will-generate-152-1-billion-in-2019-as-the-u-s-overtakes-china-as-the-biggest-market/

Williams, Walt. 2017. *Significant Zero: Heroes, Villains, and the Fight for Art and Soul in Video Games.* New York: Atria Books.

Youngblood, Jordan. 2017. "'I wouldn't even know the real me myself': Queering failure in MGS2." In *Queer Game Studies,* edited by Bonnie Ruberg and Adrienne Shaw, 211–222. Minneapolis, MN: University of Minnesota Press.

Index

Printed in the United States
by Baker & Taylor Publisher Services